CASTLES IN THE SKY

A MEMOIR OF LOVE, LOSS

AND

LEARNING TO LIVE AGAIN

RUSSELL COOK

1

First Published by Rewrite Man Publishing, 2020

This is a true story though the majority of the names of the people featured have been changed.

Rewrite Man Publishing

E-Mail: russ@therewriteman.co.uk

ISBN: 9798657623437

2

CONTENTS.

FOR OSCAR AND LEO

AND IN MEMORY OF J.H.R

INTRODUCTION: EIGHT YEARS ON

Revisiting Castles in the Sky eight years after it being written wasn't an easy experience. The journal if I can loosely call it that, was written over a four month period starting a few days after Jenny's death by suicide. It continued until I felt that I had said all I needed to. I could have continued on and on but I would have been going over old ground digging away trying to find a solution to the unanswerable question. "Why?"

Why is a great word and to start a sentence with that can lead just about anywhere most likely towards insanity! Why? reverberates through every single person's train of thought who has experienced the repercussions of a suicide. It stops there; you will never get an answer that is satisfactory or can close the case. In best Detective Colombo style you will never have that satisfaction of the final scene "So tell me detective, can you explain to me how you worked out...?" It won't happen, it can't happen.

Some leave notes, leave letters, Jenny didn't. I can say with confidence though not certainty, that the day before she took her own life she hadn't then made the decision .She was anxious and struggling with the depression; however it was one of those situations that with hindsight, oh, don't you just hate that word, well we all should have seen the warning signs, she was perkier, she'd gone to the scheduled regular appointment with her therapist. Later she had met a friend for coffee. A day lived. On that fateful morning of 23rd February as I was leaving for work at 7.30am she came up to me, gave me that big hug saying "Thank you for looking after me." Something she had never done before. That's where the word hindsight becomes so annoying. I left, she saw her son off to school, and she was dead by 9.am. Yes, with hindsight....

The only way I could deal with this at the time was to write. I called the pieces my "daily whitterings" It helped, it became an obsession that took over.

I did think of publishing Castles in the Sky in 2012. I pitched the idea to various literary agents and publishers, nothing came of it and now I'm glad, it wasn't the right time. When you are immersed in your own grief you forget there are other people involved, a mother, a brother and most importantly a son.

However the story has sat with me and recently in the midst of Covid19 Lockdown madness I revisited the Castle in the Sky and found I wanted to remember an extraordinary woman who just on first meeting blindsided me. I fell in love so completely and if nothing ever happens to me like that again, I will remember that and those feelings of completeness.

Here is a story that I hope will reverberate. When someone dies the vibrancy and life of that person is extinguished to be remembered in the form of the anecdote, a story to be passed down the generations of family and friends until the final destination of the sepia enhanced photograph. A life frozen in time. Read on, I hope it explains.

PROLOGUE: HELLO AND GOODBYE.

When my phone rang at 3.05pm on Thursday 23rd February 2012 I knew that Jenny had died. I answer. "Russell, its Oscar, its Mum, she's in the bathroom and she's not moving". Oscar, Jenny's son, has just got home from school; he calls the ambulance as I stand motionless in the centre of London, looking at my phone, waiting for it to ring again, waiting for it to be Jenny, waiting for her to tell me it's all a mistake. "You twit!" Jenny laughs "of course I'm not dead! Now hurry home we are having chicken curry for tea yet again!" This doesn't happen. She doesn't tell me because she can't; the phone remains quiet as if out of respect. I walk towards the station, need to get home. Then the phone does ring. Jenny? No. I hear a lot of voices in the background, our home just a few minutes ago so very quiet, now a hive of activity. It is Andy, Jenny's brother, I'm relieved in a way Oscar has called him, called his Gran, a thirteen year old boy who has just found his mother dead. Andy pauses mid sentence listens to someone, a paramedic next to him, I pick up the conversation, Andy confirms. "Yes, she's dead." "Oh okay" I say, so polite. "I'll see you when I get back" spoken as if I am just popping out to the shops for a few essentials, I hang up. I walk to the train, I feel constricted my suit is clinging to my skin. It's hot, the train is crowded as the over ground journey starts, scenery flashes past at a record pace but I see everything from the window. Lives being lived, school runs, laughter in the park, the race to the end of the day as my train takes me to, to…. No, this isn't real! The day before was real what I am seeing from the train window is real, but what has just happened? We were together just a few hours ago, yes, just a few hours before…..

I have to leave the house early this Thursday. Work is important and I can't be late. I wake and just before getting up I gently touch Jenny's hand, she seems tense almost brittle, probably the deepness of her sleep. I get out of bed tiptoeing out of the room so as not to wake her; she needs sleep lots of sleep. I fill the kettle and it whooshes into life as I go back upstairs to shower and shave. I creep back into our bedroom and rescue some clothes that were chucked casually on the floor last night, "naughty!" I think as I pick up socks, pants but do rummage in the wardrobe for a clean shirt and grab my suit from behind the door. I get dressed in the bathroom leaving Jenny to sleep until the inevitable wake up of the 7.am alarm. I make cups of tea and take one up to Jenny, she stirs as I gently brush back her hair from her sleeping face, "Morning" I whisper and creep out of the door and get ready to leave.

As I unlock the back door I hear footsteps on the staircase. Jenny, wrapped up in her grey fluffy dressing gown walks towards me. "Hi" she says with a half smile moving past me towards the toaster. Time to prepare Oscar's breakfast. The beginnings of the school day for him. "Good" I think. "She is up and getting on with her day. She is functioning. Must go, work is important, always so important." the thoughts cascade forward towards the commute. Fresh from putting on my jacket I walk up to her as she prepares Oscar's breakfast. "Right then, see you later, are you okay?" She again half smiles but doesn't say anything. I pull her close and we hug. "Look if there is anything you need just let me know, just phone or text?" she nods, we kiss but we only catch each other's cheeks like two uncoordinated people in a rush. Off I go, leaving her to the day ahead; I don't look back and stroll purposely to my car. Must go, work is important, always so important. Later battling the vagaries of rush hours, traffic jams and delayed trains, I text Jenny at 9:06 am "How are you doing?" No reply. I think nothing of it….. or to the text sent at 1.46pm, "Day going ok?"

I am back in the now as my reflections are brought to a juddering halt by the train stopping. I am at Twickenham station. I need to get off; need to get to the car and home. Walking purposely through the barriers and across the road past the post office and in the direction of the rugby stadium, I keep reality at bay as my last words to Jenny haunt me, one foot in front of the other one word in front of another, "just phone or text" It is so easy to keep in touch these days, to be able to reach out and ask for help? Jenny, please just phone or text, empty words that can't break through the darkness that I didn't see that morning, so well hidden.

Once back at the car I sit inside with my hands gripping the keys realising that when I next stop I will be home, a home that Jenny and I had set up together just a few months before, both our sets of possessions becoming intertwined to create a little castle in the sky for us as we talked excitedly of our dreams and plans in the years that would inevitably follow. Sure a done thing! Together always together hand in hand we were invincible eh?

I navigate the A316 leading on to the M3 concentrating hard but I feel my hands start to shake as I grip the wheel tightly. The last time I remember them shaking is when I stepped out of my car and approached Jenny's Mum's house on a very crisp winters' evening many many days before. A first date between two consenting adults who had known each other for a good few years. A first proper date without anyone else around. Jenny and me on our own. She has been really unwell and completely unable to look after herself or Oscar so at her Mum's. Definitely not a teenage date whilst still living with the parents! No, this is December 2009, I am 43 Jenny is 44 but despite our ages giving way to a little life experience, I feel like a lovesick teenager as I negotiate the icy pathway to her Mum's front door. I arrive on the threshold, the door opens and there she is. "Hello!" she smiles, "I'm ready, and shall we go?" this elegant dark haired woman, dressed in jeans, polar neck and wrapped up in a long black overcoat walks by my side to the car and we are away, to the cinema complex near Basingstoke and the evening showing of "Twilight: New Moon". In the car she talks of the past few months and her illness as she comes to terms with the depressive disease that nearly took her in the summer followed by the months of recovery. "I am determined to remain positive; this is not going to beat me!" I glance at her as I navigate the dark back roads towards Basingstoke, she, as if conscious of my look turns towards me I catch the

12

brightness of her sapphire blue eyes. "Hi" I say, "Hello again Russ" she smiles and her hand brushes mine. The pathways are icy in the car park and I take her hand as we negotiate the walk to the cinema entrance, tickets bought we make our way to the seats, just us and six other people. Jenny leans back in her seat and kicks off her boots pulling a bag of revels out of her pocket as she does so. Lights down and off we go into the twilight world of vampires and teenage angst. As the film slowly progresses Jenny rests her head on my shoulder and adding to the sexual tension created by the fictional Edward and Bella on the big screen I feed Jenny some revels. We munch away, lost in our own version of Twilight. I don't want the film to finish. I want to stay in this moment, enclosed away from reality finally on my own with this woman who I have known for nearly four years. A number of false starts, unanswered love letters long months of not speaking and missed opportunities and here we are. I think! Am I getting ahead of myself? As the credits roll we make our way back to the car again I hold Jenny's hand, I mean it is the gentlemanly thing to do the pathways are slippery! The drive home passes far too quickly and as we approach the village I suggest a coffee at mine. A pause that seems like a lifetime "That would be lovely but I promised Mum I wouldn't be late and..." she stops and says no more. I immediately understand. We drive to her mother's and we walk to the door. As we get there she turns to me her long dark hair glistening in the moonlight; she leans up and kisses me on the lips, her hand clasps mine as we kiss again but just on the lips. She pulls back "See you soon, please?" she whispers "Nite!" and she is gone.

I drive off and home, I don't want to leave her. I've started a journey that I am unable to stop. One I don't want to stop.

My thoughts come back to now, the now I don't want to face, I am driving home to her, always to her, but now to a memory that I don't want to see and can't imagine. This time I want to stop the journey, this shouldn't be happening. A very different sort of twilight sets in from the imaginary world of those tentative overdue beginnings. As I get closer to my present I push the twilight of now away and remember...

Remember the magical times of the end of 2009 leading into 2010; remember our friendship developing into something more, tentative arrangements becoming firm plans and shortly after New Year the snow fell, literally putting life on hold, the white blanket closing roads and the outside world for a few days. As the children played in the park with never-ending snowball fights and toboggan races, I reached out for Jenny and took her in my arms. "We are in this for the

14

long haul aren't we?" I say, this time there was no pause, no hesitation, no wasted time "Yes, yes we are" her words echoing across the silence of our snow white idyll.

I am nearing home now and the picture fades of the two of us walking through the snow hand in hand, the beginnings of a relationship that we knew would last the test of time, whatever life had to throw at us, we would face it together.

I drive along my road and I see the police car. I park and go to the front door. Should I ring the doorbell? I don't, use my key and am greeted by two policeman and a couple of paramedics both wearing gloves. I smile, they all smile back with that "Oh so sorry" look but none catch my eye. Could I give a statement? Where? It appears the house is off limits as there are things that need to be done. I end up sitting in my car talking to an officer about me, about Jenny, leaving the house this morning, the care she was receiving, how was she first thing today? I come out with that phrase I swore I would never use "We all thought she was getting better".

At the end of the statement I am tactfully told that I need to leave the house, our house for an hour as Jenny has to be...prepared. Do I understand? No, not really but I do as I am told and find myself driving again with a bottle of beer in my pocket. I

15

drive to the Ellie's house across the village. Ellie is my ex- wife and one of my closest friends we have a son together, Leo. They are all out and I sit in silence on the swing chair in the garden darkness enveloping me as the chair rocks me back and forth I sip my beer as it does so. The phone rings just as Ellie, her partner Doug and Leo arrive back armed with fish and chips. I barely give them a look as I process the call, the anonymous voice at the end of my mobile says I can come back now as Jenny is ready to go. "Where? Where is she going?!!" I think this but I don't say it as I say hello and goodbye to my extended family. My need to get back stops me asking how they are; I am soon driving again to my home. Things will be all right this time won't they? I phone Jenny's Mum Belinda and we agree to meet at the house. She wants to say goodbye to her daughter. We meet on the drive and exchange the ridiculousness of small talk as we approach my front door as if this is the most natural thing in the world. We are met by the inevitable police officer and shown into the lounge as if being ushered to the best table at the most exclusive of restaurants.

The present hits home, no time now for happy memories as soon as we entered the room they became trapped, locked away elsewhere. The key is lost as we both look down and there she is Jenny black hair pushed back, eyes closed. I watch

Belinda as she lets out a cry of pain "Oh darling I'm so sorry. So sorry for everything" The tears come. A mother presses a kiss on her daughter's still lips, more tears come. I, wrapped in my long dark winter coat feel cold, I start chewing my fingers and shaking my head feeling like a troubled child who can't get to grips with a seemingly unsolvable problem. I just stare and look. Look at Jenny, the smile has gone, the dazzling smile is no more she is still and I don't know what to do....

Belinda and I leave the house we talk, small talk, big talk, silly talk, who knows and as we stand by her car the paramedics glide silently past behind us with the trolley. I see but Belinda doesn't. Jenny is now wrapped up and going. The van drives off. Belinda goes, she has to, and Oscar is with her now at her house, with Andy as she went to see her daughter. I haven't thought about Oscar, what must he be feeling? He came home after a normal school day expecting to be greeted as always by his Mum....

Back at the house it is silent. I walk through to the kitchen there is Jenny's unwashed tea cup from this morning, the remains of Oscar's breakfast sits neglected on the side. I walk up stairs, in the bathroom sit her glasses by the bath, neatly put down after the final act.

I go through to the bedroom and sit on the freshly made bed. It is so quiet I don't turn on the light but pick up Jenny's discarded dressing gown and hold it close. The long haul is over and I am completely lost, my head spinning with that sentence from the first date "I am determined to remain positive, this is not going to beat me!"

The next few days roll into one and a support network begins to come together rather like a spiders web hastily constructed, spreading itself across the village, then far and wide, all links leading to somewhere. The phone doesn't stop ringing then I hear Leo has had a fall! "Possible broken leg Russ, shall I meet you at the school?" says his Mum. We take Leo to A&E, all fine just bruising but Leo makes good use of the crutches he is given and we laugh at the situation and I look into his eyes and see the pain, the pain of the fall and the pain of not understanding what has happened to Jenny. He found out she had died as I was driving back from London he also had just got home from school, the same school. He talked it through with his Mum, he listened trying to understand, his first experience of a loss of life which is brutal in normal circumstances but not as brutal as Jenny's chosen departure. Two hours of counselling leading to a lifetime of self counselling as to why? We smile at each other and Leo asks how Oscar is. Will he still be living with us? A home of just a few months? I don't know. I really don't know. Leo and I visit Belinda; she and I catch each others eye both of us hiding the pain in front of the kids. Leo proudly shows off his crutches the false jollity of the grieving, Oscar is playing games on his iPad and would love to come back for tea. Later, we cook pizza and the boys laugh and joke but I drive Oscar back to his Gran. I don't know what to say and then it comes out "I'm so sorry I just want you to know that your Mum loved you so very much" I falter, I keep my composure. Oscar stares straight ahead, I continue "and I loved her very much..." I stop, one of those awful pauses "I know" he says but a reply to which statement? Three days earlier Oscar officially became a teenager, which was a fun time as his devoted mother gave him a day to remember. And Jenny is hiding the darkness and is so disturbed and desperate to end the torment on that final morning that made her have no realisation that in all likelihood the first person to find her would be her son...

The support network continues to weave its web like magic. Oscar is taken out by friends he goes swimming he goes with his Mum's close friend Gill bowling along with Leo, he is being kept occupied. Leo and I spend time at his Mum's house and she hosts a barbecue for the whole family on the Sunday, we drink we laugh, Leo cooks me a mega

burger but I eat little as I look around for Jenny...
where has she gone? I need to talk to her. I get
overwhelmed by the selfishness of my grief as I
shut the outside world, friends and family out. I
seek rest bite with the countryside and at every
available opportunity I set off on the faithful river
walk with the even more faithful Golden
Retrievers. As I walk the fields and watch the dogs
bounding across the meadow like pathways I find
myself talking to Jenny. Over the weekend a
verbal letter runs through my mind, thoughts
spilling out in a stream of subconscious, fast and
furious conversations with the afterlife. I need to
talk to her, I have to talk to her and on the
Tuesday morning at the end of February my
fingers hit the keyboard.....

AFTERMATH: LETTER TO JENNY

7:46am 28th February

Hello, its five days since you left. The house is still you and I am very much a part of you. Even as I sit here at the desk I am waiting for you in that fluffy grey dressing gown to squeeze past "Sorry, sorry!" as you make your way to the kitchen... Oh, to break off for a second the song playing on the radio is by Keane, Bend and Break and the lyrics are resonating in my head, pounding away "I'll meet you on the other side, I'll meet you in the light, if only I don't suffocate I'll meet you in the morning when you wake." Should I laugh? Suppose so. Yes to make your way to the kitchen for that refreshing cuppa. You don't and the cup remains resolutely in the cupboard and Winnie the Pooh still has his head stuck in the honey pot. Do you think he'll ever get out? Does he want to?

I miss you. I don't know why you did what you did, I will never understand but again I do understand; does that make any sense? I was very hurried in my good bye to you on that day, conscious that I had to get to London it was a rushed hug and peck on the cheek as I stepped out into the near dark morning with a reminder for you to put the bins out. You nodded and I rushed up the path through the wooden door to the car not looking back to give you that final wave. Earlier in our brief conversation I had told you to text or call me. Why? I didn't know but I wanted you to get the reassurance to get though another day and I would be home in the evening, chat, dinner and a curl up on the sofa with the knowledge that I would be home on Friday, and then it would be the weekend.

As I write this I'm thinking of the Leisure Centre and when we used to meet in the coffee shop viewing gallery area. Not sure why but I have this strong image of you sitting there watching the boys swimming, I would come in fresh with the showery sweat of the gym; there you would be turn to me smile stand up and hold out your hand, oh the warmth of your touch and caress, to be together, watching the silent splashes of the swimmers; coffee sipped both of us realising how uncomfortable those seats were, we always sat there though.

Well, I'd better get on I've got to go to Andover today and do some bits. I will write again later. Sorry but you can't get rid of me that easily!

2.38 pm 28th February

I've just got back from Andover. I didn't realise how hard this was going to be. We were there just a few weeks ago, remember? There you were in Wilkinsons and I get the excited phone call that Lynx shower gel was on offer which ones did I like how many should you get?!! I walk past the store and up the high street and my legs turn to stone and I get tightness in my chest. Oh Jesus this isn't real is it? I turned back to look towards the store to expect to see you running out and smiling, bag full of goodies. Of course you don't and you never will. The only image I have in my mind is of you walking upstairs last Thursday morning.

"THIS IS NOT HAPPENING, YOU ARE STILL HERE!!" internally my voice was crying this out "WHERE ARE YOU, PLEASE COME BACK. DON'T DO THIS!!" For a few moments I was very angry Jenny you did this you walked upstairs and did this!

Ok I did calm down but boy was that pain intense it came over me in a wave of absolute despair, I had feelings of pointlessness you have gone and I don't know what to do, I really don't.

Home now and the happy memories flood over and I think of us in the Andover PC World store 3D glasses on watching the 3D Sky TV demonstration. Dancing, dancing lots of dancing. That was really funny. Talk of the future and perhaps a 3D TV one day. Now we will never find out.

08.52 pm 28th February

Jenny. Family Guy has finished, the DVD box set arrived yesterday, I was in when the postman arrived so no having to drive to Winnall to pick up the package. Oscar and Leo had pizza for tea followed by far too much Ben and Jerry's, but a treat is a treat. Your Mum has been great she pressed £20 into my hand when I picked Oscar up to buy tea. He hasn't been to school for the past couple of days, it will take him a while, he misses you but doesn't express that although he finds the night times difficult, far too much time to think I suppose. He is doing well though and I will do what I can to keep your memory for him as the loving devoted mother that you were.

I feel selfish for thinking about me. I think about me when I think about you and that is all I do, think about you my you the beautiful you that I fell in love with in the playground six years ago. I don't want your memory to fade, that is all I have the memory of you, it was all so short and I want us to be as we were, to see your smiling so beautiful face. I want to curl up with you in bed and feel your breath on my lips as you drift off to sleep. I weep for you and the pain you were in, you should have told me let me try and save you. You trusted me I would have protected you from it all you know that. Nite.

08.33am Tuesday 29th February

I was looking in the garden first thing this morning and I've neglected the bird table. It looks a little sparse; you were so good at that keeping everything with the house up together. I have checked on the guinea pigs but I need to learn how to feed and water them I know that sounds very stupid but I've asked Oscar to give me a hand with them this morning. He hasn't gone to school again today said he couldn't and for the time being he must do as he wants. I'll let you know how he does. You know I will do my best for him.

Yesterday I reread the Cook's World pieces that I wrote for you, from the early fragility of Unrequited. Love Letter from the Heart to the more impassioned While You Were Sleeping. Actually reading them back there is still a lot of emotion in that first letter to you when we didn't know each other at all. Did I fall in love with you utterly and completely when we first met! No question marks there. I think so!! If you had let me in then would things have been different? Let's not go there. Will write later.

09.30pm 29th February

How is life with you if that is not too painful a question! Little joke there from both sides of the fence, or is that both sides of the afterlife? Another little joke there. Has it been a tough day? I think every day will be tough for the foreseeable future but I don't blame you for that. This time last week we were curled up on the sofa watching a movie, I gave you a neck massage you were tense and it relaxed you. Earlier or was it later you came up to me in the kitchen and gave me a hug and said "thank you for looking after me" Was this a final good bye? Did you know what was to happen on Thursday morning? As per usual, a little later in bed I pulled you towards me and we snuggled up for a while and as sleep took over we parted and drifted off into our separate worlds.

Do I want to turn back time on that Thursday morning? Too right! I want to look you directly in the eye and say "What are you feeling?" away with the platitudes. "What are you really feeling?" And in the reality of my imaginary little world you would have told me, I then take your hand and protect you from the darkness, determined for us together to beat this. Now a song is going through my mind "Halfway up the stairs is a stair where I sit..." I could have stopped you halfway up the stairs where I would sit patiently waiting. Still waiting, too late? Okay I take the point!

That extra day in February, number 29! The time when a woman can ask a man that oh so important question. If you were here now and asked me that question which would have resulted in confetti being thrown left right and centre! Yes, I know, you're cross at me laughing at the image of you running around tidying up after all that celebration. "What about the carpet?!" you would exclaim rushing around clearing up. I can't talk, just spilt a glass of red over the desk, and cleared up now, no need to rush over with the kitchen roll. Anyway, back to the earlier point.

Would I have said yes? To you, the most beautiful of women. If you were here, with me now? I don't honestly know but, with you not here... "Will you marry me?" Yes, absolutely, yes". Nite.

12.38pm 1st March

This time last week the house was locked up and empty and you'd done what you thought was best. There I was doing my stuff in the Hilton Hotel Olympia and your physical form was lying in the lets be tactful, colourful bath water. Still, silent, locked house, you meant it this time. Today the sun is out and I've just got back from a bike ride fresh from a little cardiovascular. As I pedalled along headphones plugged into the ears taking no notice as usual of the passing traffic, the shuffle part of the iPod let forth "Where do We Go

27

From Here" sung by the wonderful Peter Skellern. Remember? I've mentioned him a few times, my father was a big fan and many childhood weekend evenings were full of the vinyl scratching of the singer echoing through the floor as I lay in my bed trying to sleep, stopped by the laughter and the muffled clink of overfull whiskey glasses below. I think you should listen to the lyrics which sum up the first tentative days of our relationship ".... How do we know from here, how do we decide, is this love when you were near that aches and aches inside." You were so nervous worried that you would hurt again. When we first started spending time together and it was clear that there was no turning back I could sense that feeling of "Should I?" You said yes and we did and that was such a happy day as we battled the cold of Bournemouth beach and you asked if you could wrap your arm through mine, I never let go...well lets go back to the song. "... where do we start... how do we decide... is this forever, a day or a year or only now...?" For me it will always be now. It is physically over but you know where we go from here you always did.

Do check out the song, it will make you smile, check out "Afterlife.co.uk" see if you can order it up on line and get the celestial post to fly you over a copy. Sorry a little irreverent humour so early in the day.

I've been looking at some photos and found the Brighton ones, you sitting on that wall on the edges of the stone covered beach each there with our Morrison's Salads, you've got that sardonic look on your face "don't" as the digital camera does its work. There you are mouth full of cous cous (that sounds weird but strangely interesting!!). It's a lovely moment and one of many happy days. Brighton was always such a joy when you were with me. Oh Christ, miss you more than I can ever express so will go for a bit and have another bike ride. Got to pick up some lasagne sauce for the tea. Have fun!

8.49pm 1st March

Another busy day. I had a couple of wobbles. I went out cycling earlier and ahead of me one of the country lanes I saw a powder blue Ford Focus whizzing ahead of me and I thought it was you! You see I remember every time I saw you when we were not together and in between the various times when we did meet, whether it was a glimpse of you as I was driving along. I even remember in Sainsbury's in the city centre, I was working in there as a Team Manager, in charge of the promotional work back in 2007 and I saw you buying some cleaning products (why am I not surprised by this?) I was at the top of the store, you at the bottom near the checkouts. Yep, every sighting I remember. I'd better be careful we are getting into stalking territory here! Every sighting, every smile, embarrassed waves from the car after I'd sent you that love letter…. So back to the Ford focus, needless to say it wasn't you; anyway you don't have that car anymore.

I want to talk of Love Letters again, to go back to the pieces I wrote about you for Cook's World. I've looked at them yet again, sorry to labour the point. As I said, it has been a while since I read Unrequited: Love Letter from the Heart but on this revisit the emotion is so raw, I just can't get over that, I really wasn't aware of it at the time. I was convinced that was it for you and me, that stop start and it was over. I'd tried but you felt your destiny was elsewhere. In your letters to me since you have confessed you had also suppressed the feelings. How silly we were, how much time we wasted. Remember how we used to joke about that first meeting and that walk back from the school playground that I never wanted to end? How I should have taken you home that day and never let you go? You would have had me arrested!

Back to the wobbles. I was late for Leo's school open evening, there I was huffing and puffing to meet up with Ellie and Leo, standing outside the classrooms in the late afternoon Spring sunshine and I saw people who knew but didn't know what to say. There they were, looking at me before uttering the understandable platitude of "How are you?" Not a great deal I can say really without causing an embarrassing scene that would be the talk of coffee mornings for the terminally bored for a good few generations. Any way I had a wobble, couldn't express myself, where was I? Where am I? More importantly, where are you? Can you come home soon and give me a hug? Nite.

10:04 am 2nd March

Morning how is you today? I was in the bathroom earlier conscious that the basin is getting a little dirty, you know, normal day to day stuff. You must have cleaned that basin every day, it was always sparkling; taps that would need the bathroom visitor to wear sunglasses for any lengthy stays. So I will try and keep the house up together because when you were in charge it did look homely and I think you were happy here for those brief few weeks? Time for that moment of regret now from the me that is lost without you. If; that word which is the scourge of the well-intentioned, if I had taken on board earlier what you had said about the cleanliness, yes you were way over the top but...... if I had listened earlier? I used to always bring you flowers and you loved all

31

those roses that you proudly displayed in the vase on the sideboard but; yes but another one of those words that strikes fear into the grief of the guilty; when I came home with a four pack of cider, oops , sorry kitchen roll, you would whoop with delight. Such a cheap date!

So, back to the cleaning. I had a look around the kitchen, bits on the floor, residues of my cooking prowess, thought best to give the floor a little whizz with your compact Black and Decker dustbuster. It's plugged in behind the tumble dryer and the cord doesn't stretch that far. So, despite the obvious disadvantages before I switch it on I gave it a go. Well, it made a noise and seemed to be sucking well (now really, not one of your pretend "shocked" smutty looks please!) but the breadcrumbs and assorted dust particles are still there. Hmm, I had a look at the nozzle and gave it a shake. No good. What am I doing wrong? If you could send me a quick text… still waiting. No ping. Hello? Ok you've made your point. I'll get the trusty vacuum out. Enjoy your day.

12:06 pm 2nd March

I'm really missing you now. I've done the usual things gone through the linen basket looked at the clothes that you last wore on the day before you left. I'm feeling lost in the house, really lost. Best go out for some exercise. I will be back later.

13:57 pm 2nd March

It really has been an odd day so far. The days actually go really quickly whether they are odd or not. I was upstairs earlier when the doorbell rang. Thinking it was someone to talk about you; I quickly finished brushing my teeth, threw on a shirt (the usual blue scruffy one before you ask) and ambled purposely downstairs and waited for someone to say how sorry they were to hear of your passing. I was pleasantly surprised to be greeted by a hairy man. By hairy he had hair but it was also sprouting from his neck all the way up the line of his adam's apple, white sprouty hair as if his ears had used too much Regaine oil and sent the surplus on holiday. I say that because I had a look at his ears too. The word tufts springs to mind. Any way he didn't know you, I had no need to even ask as the first thing he wanted to know was if I listened to the radio? It appears that he wants me to listen to the radio for a week, note down the stations what times listened to etc. He is coming back tomorrow afternoon to take some details probably to find out if I'm mentally competent to switch on the radio. That should be an interesting conversation. Maybe he can't listen to the radio himself due to the sprouting, everything a bit muffled?

I was about to go out for a bit when I thought I should check on the guinea pigs. I have been watering them and feeding them to the best of my ability. They are a noisy lot, did all the water etc, turned the heating down but it took me about half an hour to get the water back onto the cage where the squeaky rodents live. I did everything to try and get that plastic thing to reconnect to the wire. I didn't curse that much, just the odd word you understand but the problem is trying to avoid being bitten by them as they emerge en masse from the cardboard tubes, hungry for the monkey nuts. I did it, no blood shed in the shed, just frustration between the cage, me and the steely eyes of the four legged fur balls.

Yeah I'm feeling very tired as I'm carrying a huge weight, rather like Jacob Marley with his chainmail, money safes and keys, constantly rotating around the days of the earth paying for his misdemeanours . Odd I know but I shouldn't be feeling like this and I feel guilty for feeling so sad and frustrated. I feel the grief is about to hit again and the word IF which I mentioned earlier is about to give me the two letter salute in spades. Time for a dog walk, perhaps do some good. Plug in the iPod. What do the celestial airwaves offer in terms of entertainment? Anything worth cloud plussing? Speak later.

09:49 am 3rd March

Sorry I didn't write last night but I was really tired, my body was saying enough is enough just for a few hours. Leo and I had jacket potatoes for tea and once we'd finished the beyblade battles and he was in bed I watched Desperate Housewives, a couple of episodes to catch up on. It was hard to watch to begin with as we always used to watch it together often in bed of a weekend morning. Anyway I'm really missing you at the moment, the hands are shaking, and I curled up in bed last night clutching your purple polar neck sweater, the one you were wearing the night before you left. It just hurts and I am now questioning what you did and I'm starting to feel really angry wanting to cry out "Why did you do it?" I know that when the blackness didn't have such a powerful grip you didn't want to leave; your devotion to Oscar always stopped you. You told me that you didn't want to go away, just not to feel the hopelessness any more. Oh Jenny I'm just really cross with you today!! That's because, nine days in I feel that I am now starting to fall apart without you; it has hit home you are not ever coming back and that makes me really MAD!! What do I do, you have to tell me! Have a think and you can let me know later. Promise?

10:31 am 3rd March

Off to football now but I'm still very cross with you! Talk later.

13:17 pm 3rd March

Leo's leg still not good enough for him to resume playing football also no rugby tomorrow, he has gone back to his Mum's for a few hours I think he is fed up hearing me talking about you all the time, the phone calls emails, Facebook messages etc. he sees my changing moods and doesn't want this to keep going on. So, he senses my sadness, looks at my blank face as I am staring off into space thinking of you, always thinking of you. When I collect him later we will have a sad free evening, are planning to do some cooking a new recipe me thinks.

I hear your name in my head continually, Jenny, Jenny, over and over again. I wake up in the night hear my inner voice going on and on. I wake on your side of the bed so immediately know you are not there, I grab your clothing towards me and hold it tight then in the silence I listen intently, for another human breath in the room apart from mine, the deep rhythmical breathing of another heartbeat. I still hope that perhaps bad dreams do last this long. This has been the worst day so far; I want to curl up in a ball (yes I know with my current physique this isn't going to happen without some dramatic remedial surgery!) and

36

hug myself to keep the pain that is attacking my emotional defences out. It was bad this morning. No enthusiasm for anything. Why am I getting up, why am I boiling the kettle? As the day goes on I pick up the papers I'm not going to read, I do the recycling and tidy house, washing up and laundry to do. And to what ends? I walk around the house on my own, just the one heartbeat, each room empty of your vitality and energy that kept me going as I wanted to make our lives better, to wake you on a Sunday morning, catch your sleepy smile and just take you in my arms and become part of you and you me. That's gone and will never come back. Forgive me that's the anger I feel now and if I'd texted you earlier on that last morning and said "don't, just wait I will take your hand and pull you back again. We can beat this" deep down I know that it isn't a win win situation. The pain for you has gone but what about the rest of us? Sorry to be so blunt but I have to understand for me and you, the beautiful you, always the beautiful you. I won't write again today. Leo needs a step away from this. Enjoy Saturday, speak tomorrow. Love you, TRULY MADLY DEEPLY.

08:12am 4th March

Morning, I've just got up well it is easy like a Sunday morning. I was lying in bed watching Scooby Doo and chillin'. I had my first dream about you last night. You weren't technically in it but there was I trying to get back home and to you. I was on a boat rushing to get to a connecting airport for a flight to Gatwick and I had about 25 minutes to get to check in. On the way I bought with some small change a raspberry flavoured Mars Bar, I was on a boat at the time, don't make any sense dreams do they? The image I had in my mind was of you in a photograph just smiling a photograph of you from 20 years ago big blue eyes that didn't look tired just full of life and that smile! You are so beautiful, happy and wanting to get on and enjoy life. As I struggled to get to check in this photograph was in my mind. I knew I had to get back to you, I could feel the presence of you but we never spoke. Why the photograph this searing image of happiness implanted in my dream like subconscious? Yesterday your Mum came over with Andy to collect your car. It is signed over to her now. She had some photographs for me to look at, as she thought she had found one that can be used on the order of service for your funeral. Oh, if you are free Monday March 12 2.45pm Basingstoke Crematorium. Okay? And there was you the image that had fought its way into my sleepy dreams. At your Mum and Dad's home in this very village a family Christmas this big beautiful carefree smile. Wow! It took my breath away. I always called you my beautiful lady but even I wasn't prepared for

38

this! We all looked at this photograph and several others of the happy carefree you. Why Jenny? You did have so much to live for. Silly girl. Anyway, your Mum has the car; she has been brilliant and is grieving as only a mother can. Time for you to let the feelings go now don't you think? Andy just smiles and despite being in your Mum's shadow misses you so much he stutters with his feelings wanting to say more than he can. Oscar has just spent a couple of days with Avril and her niece Caroline. Avril, who really was your Mum's best friend full of support and in her unique way, knows what to do.

You and I both know what The Black Dog means. How many articles did we read on the subject! However I am now battling with The Black Sock. You would never let me near the washing machine so I wasn't quite sure how it worked. I wasn't about to get mine out of the garage and start swapping them over so when the washing pile began to get a little unmanageable thought it best to give it a go. If all else fails go to wash number four on the spin cycle. Works for me and it did! So underwear has done, shirts, my battered shorts. The problem is despite having washed all the socks I am now left with six odd black socks, they sit on the table by the window alone; they have lost their partners, mismatched, the poor man's footwear. Now when you did the washing this never happened, you matched them together, all folded neatly away in the sock draw or in the cupboard. Can you tell me how? It was all second nature to you, just like you were to me.

Leo and I had Chicken Zorba last night. Worked from a recipe card and produced a lovely dinner. Later we watched enjoying some episodes of Mrs Brown's Boys. The first series which we never saw. The last time I saw you properly laugh was watching the episode where good old Mrs Brown accidently took the LSD then came downstairs dressed as Wonder Woman. For a moment your dark eyes lit up and the pain went away. I think back to the photograph. Will anything I do not remind me of you?

It's raining today, first proper rain since you left. My cousin Iain is coming over as is my sister Liz so looks like a pub lunch is on the cards. It being technically the Lords Day anything special happen on the other side of the pearly gates? Actually are we getting ahead of ourselves here? Are you still in Limbo until you have been put to rest? Never thought about that. Do let me know. One tap for yes, two taps for No? I'm listening………. What does hearing no taps at all mean?

10:22 am 4th March

I've got to wash the bed linen. I would like to point out that it is not that bad, the linen is not curling at the edges or so brittle that the assorted sheets and duvet covers could be used as windbreakers in extreme back garden weather conditions. So, about to go and strip the bed and put them into the spin cycle which will wash away the indentations of your sleep. Needs to be done but I'm still clinging on to the purple glittery polar neck. My comfort blanket to take away the silence of the night.

09:01pm 4th March

Not much to say tonight, then again I have lots I want to say to you, never ending. It's been a hard day to be honest; shall we just leave it at that? Okay, you have nothing to say? Leaving me on my own as I walk the streets of the city, whichever direction I looked, there you were in the past, running out of the sweet shop, happy so happy with the extra strong acid drops bought for me, up the long cobbled high street which we strolled down hand in hand so many times catch the breath of life as we go along not a care in the world, look left look right take that breath. Feel it Jenny you were alive! You could have had so much more. Now you have the silence and the eternal blackness that you....needed. Really? Truthfully? You are happy now? Well. I'm not, I miss you so

much, and so many people miss you so much. I don't know how to replace the you. It hurts Jenny and I'm empty and so drained the pain as the tears begin to stream down my face. We were so right for each other and you should have trusted me more. I could have done it, pulled you back…..
WHY??

09:45pm 4th March

Sorry, a bit over the top there, you see the emotions are raw and I truly truly love you with all my heart, please believe me. I wish I had said it more, especially on that morning. Nite beautiful lady and if you had one little wish rubbing that imaginary magic lantern? Just knock on the door; I'll let you in….

08:21am 5th March

A funny night. I did the bed linen as mentioned, all lovely and scrummy, so well done by me that the duvet kept sliding off! Vivid dreams of going to the theatre to see a production of Hamlet starring David Tennant. I was leaving tea cups everywhere and having to collect them. Again I was on my own as I slurped tea from half drunken mugs around the seaside based theatre. I did have a restless night, thoughts of you and the conversations I still want to have. I am playing again and again our final conversation on your last morning. The way I want it to go? In my parallel world I am looking you directly in the eye "How are you?" I say. I get through the fog of the black eyes, you can barely speak as the darkness is willing you on to take that final journey but I push it back, gather you up and hospital, someone to watch over you and we try again. What do you think? Worth a try?

I bet you get stressed when you are looking at the house and me pottering around. "Are you going to do the washing up today?" I can hear you now! "Make sure you take those shoes off before you step on the carpet!" See, wherever your final journey ended and the peace so long craved washed over the tormented soul and the darkness ebbed away, you would have encountered one final drawback. No more house cleaning! You can't do anything about it! The fabrize is out of your reach and on choosing your destiny you gave up your rights to the kitchen roll! Sorry, those are the breaks. The kitchen roll is now mine! Will I ever buy another bottle of fabrize again? This must be torture for you. Thinking things through and not able to squeeze another bottle of fairy liquid? One day when the pearly gates welcome me and we meet again, look out for the man in the blue scruffy shirt and raincoat looking nervous and confused. Red rose in hand? Glasses of red wine for me and you? For me to see your beautiful smile again, I know, you don't have to tell me, antibacterial hand wash it is! Speak later. Off for a cuppa, yes I've used the Brita water filter, the kettle is still scale free!

06:07pm 5th March

It's been a really tough day as I am trying to come to terms with you as you and what you were to me in the times after we met and when we got together. Because you know as well as I that we should have been together from day one. If I had been there from day one in 2006 you would have been better I know that. You kept telling me that, all obvious obstacles aside! It gnaws away at my subconscious. I'm sorry I have had to say this it is painful but it is not with the benefit of hindsight I say this because you and I had the conversation on several occasions. I need to put those ghosts of conversations past into context so I can keep on loving you in the way you deserved and the way I did when you were here. And as I said to you as we walked along Sandbanks beach on Monday 28th December 2009, our carbon footsteps forging forward the beginnings of our relationship "Look, you need someone to treat you as you and with respect, emotionally, intellectually and physically" You gave me a big smile that day and I couldn't stop gazing into your sapphire blue eyes! Gosh how poetic that sounds! Actually it was bloody freezing on the beach, those ice cold waves crashing around us and the sand whipped up into a frenzy in the winter winds, we had to shield our eyes. I think I stood by my comments and treated you as you, the lady that you are.

09:43pm 5th March

Another evening that has passed with the phone ringing, landline and mobile, texts etc and I've got nowhere! So we will have to leave our next discussion about the troubled times when we weren't getting on until tomorrow. I hope you understand. I am happy to keep you on a pedestal and worship you from afar but this needs balance. Who am I kidding! You couldn't be further away than you are now! Nite.

09:43am 6th March

I had a dream that my computer had been taken away, just to be repaired you understand but I panicked as I couldn't look at Letter to Jenny. Without Letter to Jenny and my other scribbling I would be a little lost, a lot lost actually. It hasn't been the easiest of mornings so far, I had breakfast news on in the background and they had a group on who were all happily talking about depression and how therapy helped, even with medication a course of classes can save the day! Absolutely, did you a lot of good didn't it! I was watching the programme looking at the smiling faces of the cured. Step forward Jesus to debunk the feeding of the five thousand.

We have to tackle this you and me. I spend every waking moment wishing you were here, I am constantly searching for signs of you and hate it as the house subtly changes and your personality begins to diminish, a moved plate, a realignment of the furniture, the open windows bringing new life into our home, the breeze pushing the past times away so I have to get the balance. I have to remember the times when I would deliberately delay coming home in case you were in a bad mood when the illness had its tightest grip. A late visit to the gym, a pointless trip to Tesco? I didn't want the tension; I thought then that I wanted an empty house somewhere to relax and not to think. Worried that Leo leaving a toothbrush in the basin would provoke that late night conversation about shoes on the floor, toilet seat up. Trivial to me, very important for you. How I wished that sometimes you would not be there, but, oh that word again, but we got though it toothbrushes and basins stopped being bedfellows, shoes did remain by the door and I began to want to see you in our house and we all four of us began to laugh and actually enjoy each other's company. Does it matter now that you have moved away? I have to get the full picture clear in my head and at times the feelings of our relationship coming to an end were certainly there. Those late night rows, you were so angry the lash outs and all our frustrations would come pouring out. I would get angry at your illness taking over and you would get angry at everything taking every comment however woefully constructive from me as an attack on you. The heated conversations would follow both of us in bed, keeping us as far away from each other as possible. Fitful, restless sleep and I have never felt so isolated and lonely. You? Did you remember the arguments and the terror at the back of your eyes as the illness gripped you and you lost control? I should have just moved forward kissed your fragile lips and held you close. Held you close and said "Everything will be all right, come here stay close, sleep, sleep". Of course I should, but I didn't. Now you sleep and the words will have no effect. I have the empty house, I hate the silence.

12:08pm 6th March

This is really hard today. I've started to shake again. I miss you so much, you need to be here Jenny, enough is enough now, please help me take this pain away?

08:15pm 6th March

Cooked a rather scrummy shepherd's pie tonight. I have plenty left in the fridge so let me know when you want some. I loved your reaction to my cooking; I loved cooking for you I think you liked the step back, someone doing something for you, roast beef being a particular favourite. I enjoyed the process of preparing the food often on my own until you would sidle over to me as I was stirring the gravy, give me a smile and a hug and we would quietly talk, time would stand still. Towards the end in the days before you left I would hold you close and listen to your whispered words "I'm not good Russ, not good". The beautiful blueness of your eyes blocked by the darkness that was constantly pulling you away, wanting you to leave giving you the false hope of a relief from the pain. In the kitchen, cooking the tea we would stand wrapped up together a moment in time different each day the same every day. Then, we would eat and curl up together on the sofa, as bed approached, I would pull you back and massage your neck with the gentleness of my caress you gave yourself to me your lover, protector and companion. Later as we lie in bed I rest my weary head on your chest and hold you tight. I'm home. Now the locks have been changed and I don't know what to do. Sleep well.

08:00 am 7th March

"Good morning it is Wednesday 7th March!" announces the BBC breakfast presenter. "Good morning to you too!" say I full of rather false bon viveur. I am trying to be upbeat today. It is all very well to wax lyrical about the sensations of you being here, however its not going to change anything however much I want to turn the clocks back thirteen days. So, what else has been going on in between me tapping out sensitive prose to the most beautiful woman I know? Oh, that's you by the way...

I have been spending a lot of time with Kathy and Clive; I keep bumping into them as they only live 200 yards away. Yesterday I pedalled past, the sun was out and the warmth of an early spring was felt and much appreciated, Kathy was sitting in the garden with Heinz the dog.. They are both doing a fantastic job with him and he has settled in really well. He still misses you and whenever he is out for his walk he knows where his first home was. As he approaches number 23 he scampers to the end of his lead, pulling ferociously away as he scrabbles towards the door. This should make you smile your happy little dog.

Liz came down to visit on Sunday and she, Leo and I went out to lunch in The Vine pub where we tucked into fish finger sandwiches on a cold wintery day. Earlier it had snowed for a while; we looked out of the kitchen window as the large opal shaped flakes flittered down vanishing as soon as ground was touched. Soon cleared up the cold remained as the sun came out. We went for a walk around the city after and the Cathedral grounds braving the cold, you would have enjoyed it.

Liz and her husband Paul bought me a present. A Cavalier Hiking Pole described as "Walking Poles with Character" Each pole is unique and mine is Number 18 and of a Natural type so the little Authentication Certificate says. Any way the pole is now my companion on the frequent afternoon dog walks much to the initial delight of Olivia the snow white golden retriever who looked at my pole (careful!) as if it was the Sticky Stick to beat all Sticky Sticks! I wouldn't let her have it, had to stride along with it thrust out in front of me away from the jumping dog. To the casual passer by I must have looked like Moses striding forth for his pivotal meeting with the Burning Bush! Anyway Olivia soon lost interest and all thought of Burning Bushes could be dispelled. Quite a long hike from the Easton Field to Mount Sinai. Hope all is well with you; do get in touch when you are ready. My mobile is never switched off and it's amazing what and iPhone is capable of! Speak later Jenny.

03:18pm 7th March

Hi, I have just spent a very pleasant hour with your Mum talking about you, she was lovely and her love and the pride she feels and will always feel for you shone through. She gave me a couple of 10x8 photos of you taken in the early 1990s. Wow, just beautiful you were/are/ will be, delete as applicable. I think in this ongoing letter to you that word and I will say it again beautiful, will be cropping up many times. I am going to scan them and print them off on photographic paper. If they don't come out well then will take them to a photo shop and get them copied. "Such a waste Jenny" I thought as I pedalled the country lanes, tears streaming down my face. Easy when cycling, if people see you then you can blame the watery complexion on the incoming cold winds. Saves a lot of explanations. The only drawback of spending time with your Mum I always leave smelling of cigarette smoke. Cough, splutter, that's got it. Hope your day is going well.

08:33 pm 7th March

Good day and bad day, memories of you flood over me wherever I go or wherever I am. Here's a funny thing. I popped into Tesco tonight to pick up a couple of bits. Odd how things sometimes go, I walked past the flower section at the front of the store. I looked at the roses and immediately thought "Jenny would like…" yes I stopped myself in mid thought. I could see your thank you smile as I ushered you into the kitchen to see the bunch freshly left on the side for you to prepare and settle into the vase as only you could. It's going to be a long time isn't it? The stabs of self-realisation that really, you are not here anymore. Nite.

07:48am 8th March

Morning, hope all is well with you. I've just been scrambling around trying to find a new bin liner. This time two weeks ago you were saying goodbye to your son in more ways than any of us could ever imagine, then you did the washing up and emptied the bins. In that time I was on the M3 making my way to London.... What is that oft used phrase "Hindsight is a wonderful thing?" Well I'm not feeling particularly wonderful this morning. Speak later. Love you. Oh, found the bin liners!

09:37 am 8th March

This is really hard today. Part of me is still expecting for you come downstairs for a cuppa and give me a hug as I sit here working. I hate this. This is awful, why is it getting worse? I miss your physicality and just you, I curl up in bed at night always wake to the silence of you not being HERE!! Please don't go away!

09:07 am 9th March

Within minutes it is nearly 24 hours since I last wrote! What difference a day makes? Not much really. Not writing makes me feel as if I've deserted you. I did struggle yesterday morning the sun was out again and I pedalled the country lanes before getting ready to go to Poole to see Mum. Just as I was leaving I bumped into Sheila who was just leaving Kathy's having dropped off some photographs with her and Clive. Sheila the fragile soul that she is walked slowly towards me and gave me a very limp hug "I am so sorry, I don't want to intrude on your grief" Bless her she is in a state of shock over your leaving Jenny. On a Friday night a few weeks ago you met for a coffee when Oscar was at youth group. It was lovely to hear her talk of your constant kindness during your all too brief friendship. I don't think you ever realised how much you were loved Jenny, the village is in shock. Sheila gave me some photos of you from an Easter get together in 2008. I am looking at you now as you cuddle a chick in your hands, dressed in red that half smile as you look straight into the camera. Oh Jenny you will never ever stop taking my breath away...

Poole was good, I struggled with the drive. On the A31 I was cut up by a driver and immediately turned to you "Did you see that....!!?" You weren't there holding my hand as you always did, except when I had to change gear of course. God, I miss you.

Things were a little difficult when I arrived at Mum's flat. I just wanted you there and trying to say "Oh I'm fine" through gritted teeth; okay maybe I should have just let it all out but no, I'd rather talk and if the emotion takes over. My brother Stuart arrived with his daughter Mable who being nearly two got all shy with me being there! Mum took her to the park and a little later as I made my way through the park to the town centre I saw them in the distance surrounded by swans all after the bread, Mum, Mable and pushchair. She did this with me, Stuart, Liz and Leo in Poole Park, in her element as the years roll by.

I met up with my friend Lawrence for a drink and we had a jolly get together in the his local pub. As it was mid-afternoon we were in limbo time as the all-day drinkers begin to think of ordering that final glass of liver stifling tonic before the stagger home. Slowly they were being replaced by the evening drinkers, fresh from work, a quick pint or glass of wine or two. Lawrence and I moved away from the busy bar area and carried on talking. I always knew that our mutual love of Doctor Who can block out anything for a short period of time. Laughter is good for the soul and as that's all you probably all of you that is left, what does a giggling soul look like? All coy and shy? That reminds me of happy times. I've said enough sexy lady! Back at Mum's Mable had gone and we walked to the fish and chip shop and bought our tea. Talked of you, endlessly of you, my wonderful you. I talked of the time we first met and all those false starts and the ridiculousness of us pussy footing around each other when we should have been wrapped up in each other's arms. Mum was good, just letting me talk let the grief out with memories good and bad.

Home and as I drove the long roads home I thought of you with a smile on my face and a little tear in the eyes. We found something so special so good and we let it grow. We took care of each other maybe there were more rough than smooth but, oh that word again! But I love you with all my heart my Jenny, always remember.

09:06 pm 9th March

Gosh, within a minute, twelve hours since we last spoke. A more balanced day. Morning of the what if and wanting to pull you back from the brink, the hope of the happy ending and the continued walk up our own yellow brick road. It is going to be along while before I am able to put you to rest in my own mind but I had a few smiles today, it took a while and it felt good to smile, be out in the fresh air with the dogs on the Friday afternoon

55

walk co incidentally the one I invited you on, the final Friday you had with us. You didn't come as you didn't want to intrude on "my time" Bless you; I never appreciated sometimes those acts of kindness. Sleep well beautiful lady, my beautiful wonderful Jenny.

09:31 am 10th March

Morning, hope you slept well. The best night's sleep for me since you left. Leo and I cooked sausages and eggs for breakfast, Kung Fu Panda is on in the background, the washing machine is whirring away so thought I'd spend a few minutes with you catching up. A little bit of normality crept into my subconscious towards the end of yesterday and it continues this morning which is good isn't it? Thoughts of you still are at the forefront and I lay in bed for a good hour this morning thinking of our life together if you were still here. Would (hey I've moved up from the But and If to a five letter hindsight word!) you be okay? Would the tension still be here, the four of us enduring the pain creating that false atmosphere of just getting through the day? Hoping just hoping that you will get better as I try to pull you back yet again from that long sliding slippery dark slope? It affected us all and I think back to the pain of those first few weeks at

Christmas and New Year. Just a little food for thought sweetie pie.

Thinking of Christmas, we never had a proper one together. In the three we celebrated you were always at your Mum's, being looked after, the illness having taken its grip yet again. The one before last was okay, with you cooking the turkey for Oscar and me. Let's forget last year when I had taken to my bed. Sick and physically exhausted, I was in the grip of battling your illnesses, we all were. It was taking its toll and perhaps the thoughts of leaving were being sown for you.

10:01 am 10th March

Sorry about the above, I am not and never will try and distance myself from your memory and I love the happy "What, But, would, If" scenario of what we would have done in happy happy joy joy land but; as I have already said, you and I need to balance, at times Doctor the prognosis didn't look good. Sorry. Still would rather have you here though, a weekend morning you pottering around the house in your element counting your stash of kitchen roll! See you later on today.

10:50 am 10th March

Jenny, just washed some shirts, couple of buttons missing on the white one, could you have a look? Not good at the sewing me.

06:01 pm 10th March

It has been a really lovely day as I cycled along the county lanes, twice today in fact, (sorry off again!) one could smell the newly mown gardens and as I sit here at dusk with the back door open I can almost taste the fresh embers of a dying bonfire. You would love it, us sitting in the garden with cups of tea looking forward to the summer, looking forward to the future. Never plan because we have all the time in the world? Thinking of that phrase a lot because I was listening to the same titled song as I stomped through the fields with the dogs. Ah the cruelty of the iPod shuffle, not tactful with its choices as I soaked up the late afternoon sunshine. The last time I heard that song Jenny? On our final trip to Brighton and as we were leaving, on the familiar drive along the coast road we were listening to the radio and on came that little tune. Louis Armstrong at his calmest almost guiding us through the lyrics that had you gazing out of the window deep in thought, little Heinz asleep on your lap after his run along the stony beach. "Are you okay?" I said, squeezing your leg. "Fine, fine" your gaze not leaving the chilly late winter shore of the departing Brighton seafront. Deep in thought and I didn't give it enough thought.

Enough of the sadness, its dark now and Leo is on his way back pedalling into the late dusk. I was going to cook us a chicken korma but that was our last supper so not just yet.

What are you having for tea? Why not have a glass of wine? I am! A little hint, there is a chap probably not that far from where you are who is a dab hand at turning water into wine so if you're near a mountain stream or a babbling brook? Maybe have a nibble on an After Eternity mint (your favourite) and if you are still hungry that chap I mentioned earlier? He would give any supermarket's BOGOFF offers a run for their money. Any fish and bread handy! As always, you and me, later?

09:04 pm 10th March

Okay, nothing to say but plenty to say, Saturday night, Leo in bed, me on my own watching TV. Um I was just wondering; are you doing anything tonight? A little lonely me without you.... Goodnight my beautiful lady. Yes you were, my beautiful lady and for... how long a piece of string?

08:28 am 11th March

Morning sunny Sundays all round? Not really. They say this is a rollercoaster journey and yesterday perhaps I was up at the top of the ride having my own view of the scene around me and able to see the wood as I was high above the trees. I woke at 3.12 am, one of those sit up with a start wake ups. Darkness and the silence, deafening. I lay there and it was then that I knew. You're not coming back are you? The blind panic set in and feelings of utter hopelessness. I couldn't move Jenny I couldn't move... as my eyes became adjusted to the light I saw the silhouette of your dressing gown, your clothes where you left them on that morning, cuddly toys hanging from the wardrobe, on the dressing table an empty bottle of mineral water that I can't bear to throw out. Oh this is so hard, the pain washed over to me in waves and those thoughts again you are not coming back? Every sixty seconds the red digits of the digital clock moved time on another minute, soon 3.40am then past 4.am tick tock tick tock in silence and with dawn approaching, another day began to prepare its itinery. I have another day without you because you are not coming back.... At the moment as I write that is a little too much and the loneliness is excruciating.... Today I'm at the very bottom of the ride.

10:35 am 11th March

Mike has just called for Leo; they have gone off cycling, two near teenagers off on an adventure. A good thing as I am not at my best still but will get better, promise, Leo needs the support of his father. More washing done and an increase in odd socks, the black ones again. Any ideas?

8:42 pm 11th March

Tough day but enlightening day, sunshine in the sky to hide the showers that pervade within me. That stab of pain in the night brought the panic and I still can't believe that we will never talk again. Of an evening, those hushed confidences, the scuttle into the kitchen, the opening and closing of the cupboard and the smiling you would return with the once hidden bag of minstrels, holding my hand, you proffer me the packet, we munch away like we used to do in the anxious early days, instead of the darkened groves of the cinema lanes we are curled up in our home on the sofa at the mercy of the TV planner. Shame we couldn't have done more for us Jenny, shame that something prevented you from turning to me in those final days and just asked...

I am so lonely here without you. I have to make a journey starting tomorrow to push past the memories that I don't want to go but will eventually hold me back if I don't allow them to mature and go. I know that you wouldn't want

61

that, at the moment I see no future without you. It is up to me to challenge and defeat that. You would want me to, but, the thought of no more hellos or steamy early morning goodbyes with us locked together is for now too much to bear. Nitey nite.

10:38pm 11th March

Time for bed in a minute, don't want to go, then it will be tomorrow.

07:52am 12th March

Morning. Am feeling very nervous, sitting alone in the house. We will be in the same room again later, for a short while, not sure what to do Jenny, I need you to hold my hand and guide me through this.

09:21 am 12th March

Jenny, I've just reread yet again While You Were Sleeping. Boy I meant all that and you didn't listen, its all there Jenny what I think about you and what we could have done together. It really hurts today and I'm shaking. I know you are not coming back but please please try.....?

09:55 am 12th March

Slowly getting ready for the farewell. I'm going to wear the Mr. Perfect underpants that you bought me for Valentine's Day! Mr. Men badges on coat of course, that will make you smile. Don't need to use the word hope do I!

11:10 am 12th March

Just back from a cycle ride, helps clear the thought processes; off to buy some flowers. Perhaps a single red rose, maybe just a single red rose. A kiss from a rose… see you in a bit, won't be long.

12:30 pm 12th March

Hi, back from Sainsbury's. Memories of you as I walked around the store, our trips to do the weekly shopping, searching out the bargains, you helping me with my calls. Then I glance over at the DVD section and today the fourth part of the Twilight saga is released. We had our first "date" watching the second one when I fed you chocolates in the darkness of the Odeon that crisp winter's night back in 2009. We never got round to seeing the fourth in the cinema… reminders everywhere I look, everywhere I go, for now and a long time. Better get a move on, need to say my goodbyes to the physical you. I'm sitting here shaking and don't want to leave the house. Can you take my hand for one final time?

13:02pm 12thMarch

Now dressed and ready to go. I want to scream and shout I have tears pouring down my cheeks, Jenny why?

10:23am 13th March

Morning, so the day after? Ashes to ashes dust to dust. Those curtains that to me drew a close on your physical life and took you away, I couldn't stop looking at them all through the brief twenty minute goodbye to family and friends. Look I will talk to you about it all later. Iain stayed the night and we are off for a walk soon meeting up with Molly and their new dog Murphy. A stroll through the water meadows, you would have liked that. So much more to say later.

07:50am 14th March

So the day after the day after? Sorry that I wasn't in touch yesterday, I was out most of the day, Iain stayed for the morning, Molly joined us and we went for the aforementioned walk in the meadows which took us through to Winchester where in the Cathedral grounds we ate pasties before the walk back. As I said you would have enjoyed the walk, there was so much that we both enjoyed that we never did together enough. Anyway, moving on or rather moving back a couple of days to your official departure. I drove to village and left the car there before walking to the pub to meet up with everyone. It really was a beautiful day beautiful lady. I bumped into Pam in the pub, "How was it?" she enquired "I'll let you know in a couple of hours" I replied half smiling. Poor Pam didn't know what to say! Anyway, with all the family there including Leo tucking into a huge open sandwich, dressed in black including leather jacket. He looked really cool! I went with Iain in the van on the drive to your final goodbye, I had composed myself by this time, picked myself off the floor so to speak, no sobbing over the loss of my beautiful girl as I struggled with the cufflinks and the oversized shirt earlier in the silence of our home. Then the reality of Basingstoke Crematorium. We drove up the tarmac drive past babbling brooks and fountains all set as the centrepieces of the mini gardens of remembrances. The car park slowly filled, friends, family members,I so many coming to say goodbye to you Jenny, coming to say goodbye to you so very early. Your Mum arrived with Andy and Oscar who was immaculately turned out to say goodbye to his Mum. We all chatted, hugs, kisses and handshakes broken by the forced laughter of the repressed emotions. Then you arrived in the gleaming hearse, gliding forward towards the chapel your physical form near the end of its final journey. I wanted to go over and say hello, surely this Game for a Laugh scenario was going to come to an end as you leapt from the coffin all smiles, brushing back your tousled hair, "Surprise everybody!!" No? Okay then I'll continue back in the reality but not the reality of what any of us wanted.

Moment of truth "Everybody ready?" said the kindly respectful funeral director, the walk into the chapel for everyone, then you followed by us, Oscar, Andy and your Mum. I placed two red roses on the coffin, Oscar a single yellow rose. Kisses from us in the form of the flowers of life. We walked in to the processional music of Queen and "We will Rock You" Typical you! Quite right too!

Twenty minutes to say goodbye. In Loving Memory of Jenny said the order of service. "Is that you?" I wanted to say looking at the photo of the smiling happy lady looking out at us, clear eyed with the smile to melt the frozen paths of even the coldest of winter's mornings. Remember?

 Long time family friend Simon did the best job at guiding us to say goodbye to you. As he said in his opening comments he had known you before you were born. With great love and care he touched on all aspects of your life early days as an RAF child through school, nursing and your times as a mother and devotion to Oscar. We prayed, we sang and the times of reflection and with the precision of a well-rehearsed stage show we were led towards the committal and the curtains closing on the physical you. Jenny enough tears were shed in that chapel of supposed rest to put out even the fiercest of flames. So as you went off towards the fiery furnace, one little teardrop from any of us could have extinguished the inevitable and you could have come back. A quick script rewrite? A tweak here, an added scene there and we family and friends could grab you by the hand and we could stroll across the fields and see the dawn of a new day? I can't believe I'm saying goodbye to you, I can't believe I stood in a Garden of Remembrance and watched the tears stream down your Mum's face down your son's face as we looked at the flowers. Leo came up and gave me a cuddle he had been trying to get my attention for a good ten minutes after the service ended, it hit him really hard, he realised that you had finally gone, no more early evening helps with those tricky homework questions as you patiently guided him through the complexities of obscure maths problems. He sobbed through the service and looked utterly lost after, we hugged, his half smiles saying he was fine, he wasn't, stuttering his words through the shock he was feeling. He deserved more attention than he got from me Jenny.

Home to change, your favourite colourful tie removed Mr. Men badges put away and I slipped into my brown leather jacket, always a favourite of yours. Back to the pub for soggy sandwiches and overripe pork pies and happy talk of you, everyone full of funny stories of you, close friends June, Debbie, Kathy, coming up to me and telling me the inevitable "She really did love you, you were the love of her life, you were the one". I don't know any more Jenny I really don't know what to think. This is so selfish of me but I need to know, If that is the case why did you do what you did and walk away from your new home, your son, your family and friends and me, yes me? Have you any idea? I now lie awake at night filled with anxiety and despair hugging your sweater clinging on to the final memories of you. I'm frozen in fear for the future without you and I don't still know what to do!

These thoughts scream through my brain and as the pub emptied and everyone slowly drifted back to their day to day routines being replaced by the early evening drinkers getting on with their lives, I stood there looking at the tables being cleared away of the remaining food and half drunk cups of tea and coffee. A life's remembrance ending up being tipped into the over used kitchen bin. You've gone now and all I want to do, really want to do is sit at home curled up with you. How do I get through this beautiful lady? I have to get past the drawn curtains, please reach out and reassure me once more? Please.

Morning. How is your life in the afterlife going, have you settled in yet? I had quite a positive day yesterday; it always helps when the sun is out, cycling, cycling, more cycling, dog walking, and writing to you. It is easy to watch the days pass in the blink of an eye, sometimes it is quite nice to watch the days pass in the blink of an eye. I know that you have now gone and will not be coming back but I still feel that I have been abandoned by you. I listen to your friends telling me how "I was the one" for the first time in your life you felt you were in an equal relationship. I wish you had told me, how secure you supposedly felt, and then the blackness, the "I don't want to be here" scenario took over and on that lonely morning three weeks ago…

One lonely morning for you and lonely mornings now set in stone for your loved ones. This morning I am feeling very alone, you are not here and whatever has happened it just feels wrong, very very wrong. The ache of missing you physically and emotionally is intense, in many ways I wish it would just go away. I know I have to get on with life, go to the bank, sort the finances out (sorry, you have left me in a bit of a mess!) get a better job with a better salary. They say money is the root of all evil, not so sure about that! This all needs to be done but I'm sitting here again feeling exhausted, legs like lead, heavy head and to blow all the positives that I need to do out of the water, I just want you back! I need to wake up in the Groundhog Day mode and find a way to change the pattern of the day, the familiar day that if I am not careful will bring me down.

I don't want to go back to my life of three years ago before we got together, was I content then? I wasn't looking for a relationship, I'd put you away, compartmentalised you, a bittersweet memory that didn't work out. I had my life with Leo and we just got on with it, then you came along, I let the old feelings flood back and it was the best thing I ever did but, now? Would I have missed any of our time together? No. I wish I had held you more, I wish I had kissed you more; I wish we had just done more. I wish I had told you I had loved you more. That's four wishes, is there a lamp handy, give it a little rub? I know I am one wish over but...

Time to get on with the day, I need to get on with the day, speak later. Love you.

10:34am 14th March

Thinking of you, ten days before you left there we were in the leisure centre playing Badminton with Leo. I remember the hushed conversation before we went on court, the anxiety in your eyes as you were so struggling to cope. I gave you a hug, you gripped me tightly and we went on to play, much to the relief of my son who was waiting, badminton racket in hand. You enjoyed the game remember? We took it in turns to play Leo beating us both! I miss you, you have no idea.

08:48 am 15th March

Another day and it doesn't get any easier. I struggle with the complete lack of interest in anything apart from thoughts of you and what could have been. Vague moments of clarity if I'm writing or out in the sunshine. I am haunted by images of you on that final morning and the walk up the stairs with the knife, running of the bath and you being so tidy, slippers in the bedroom dressing gown that you were wearing hung back in its place behind the bedroom door. On your own, so on your own and the chaos in your head making you unaware of what you were doing? What would have happened if at the moment of decision I had walked in the door? Would you have stopped? A pause as a reason for you not to do it presented itself? Curtains of blackness parting as I become aware of what you were doing and I pull you back taking you in my arms. It plays over and over in my head like a stuck record, the scratching of the jumping needle getting louder and louder as internally I scream at you not being here. You not being here is just a little too much at the moment.

I can pause and look around our house, the home that you had made ours, subtle changes each day that you were here. You had so much to live for Jenny, so much. Now the house is stuck in time, everything the same but somehow different.

I write this with the guilt of the unintentionally selfish. Tragedy invades the headlines at the moment, other people are suffering much more and I still can't break out of this habit, waiting for you to walk downstairs with that first half asleep good morning smile a kiss and a cuppa. What could be better?

Oh some news you will be pleased with. Oscar has started going back to karate and has achieved his brown belt. He is as proud as you would have been. He is doing okay you know. Doing okay. Anyway have a good day. I have some things to do today, must get on, I hope! Speak later.

07:17pm 16th March

Good day? I've had a better day, much better. To work or not to work? To be with you or not to be with you? Yes or no to those two ponderous questions? I don't want to go back and have resisted it but practically if I chose or chose not to go back I will add a few more problems to the melting pot. I am on the defensive when it comes to work because I couldn't really care less. I am not interested! I know now that there is more to life and on a learning curve with you taking centre stage which you will for quite a while. However, the bills have to be paid so after a rather fractious conversation with various managers I am back clocking up the miles and spouting my own unique brand of training speak as of Monday, just three and a half weeks since you left. Do I need more time, to stay at home and think about you, preserve and protect my memories of us? Maybe but (Oh! that word) I could easily turn into a rather rugged male version of Miss Havisham flitting about the house in a flurry of anxiety and bitter wasted opportunities or worse, develop a Queen Victoria fetish and spend the rest of my life in mourning dressed in black and bursting into tears at the sight of a fir tree whether at Christmas or not. This is not going to happen; I'm not ready for a meeting with the men in white coats just yet! I know you would not want that, you always wanted the best for me for Leo your friends and especially Oscar though often neglecting yourself. And, we know what that lead to.

08:45 am 17th March

Hope all is well with you. After the positivity of yesterday, I have sunk to the bottom again, hardly any sleep and I'm here on my own on an overcast and miserable day. The rain is pouring down; due to pick Leo up for football soon, need to talk to you first. Really need to talk to you; it was 2.46am when I looked at the clock had been awake for a bit in that mode again of clinging to your sweater battling the loneliness of the silence, the loudest noise in the world, do you understand? The panic set in along with the feelings of feeling utterly abandoned. I know I know, I could pick up the phone and fill up my days with people and things to do but all I want is you Jenny. When these feelings really hit the emotional surface I just sit and wipe back the tears, tears for your actions, tears for your pain that I wasn't able to take away, tears for what we could have achieved. You stupid stupid girl! The beautiful you now just a pile of ashes, once my hand could slip seamlessly into yours our fingers entwined as we walked through life. Now just dust fragments as easily lost in the sniff of a breeze. Not right Jenny, not right. Love you….

03:25 pm 17th March

Hi, still overcast just back from a bike ride which does clear the cobwebs, sorry sweetie pie but I am still having a very bad day. Earlier, sitting with your Mum and Andy looking at you in the middle of your Mum's lounge, yep you are back for a limited time only but looking slightly different. "Do you want to see the ashes?" piped up Belinda in between drags of her cigarette. Before I had a chance to answer she flicked her ashes into her little pot before scurrying off to collect her daughter's ashes safely stored in her bedroom in an even bigger pot, away for the moment, from the sensitive eyes of your son. She opened the blue carrier bag produced a brown cardboard box which was labelled "The Cremated Remains of Jennifer. March 12th2012" I opened the box watched by your Mum and Andy. There, in a big red plastic container resembling a giant sweetie jar was a clear bag and you. Not the beautiful curvaceous you that I would make a play for at every given opportunity (gosh, do I miss the physical you...) but the departed you, ashes, a bag of ashes as if the grate from an open fire had just been cleaned. "Do you think we should pierce the bag now, just to make it easier to remove them when the times comes for the scattering?" your Mum's blunt words shattering my fireplace thoughts. I looked over at your brother. He said nothing but just smiled so I said probably not, wait for St. Catherine's Hill. I am sure Jenny you wouldn't want a little part of you trampled into your Mums carpet? You hate cigarette smoke with a passion and would rather not end up in your Mum's ash tray!

We may be doing the deed tomorrow, it is up to your son. He went out with June today along with Leo, a visit to Laser quest in Southampton. Oscar is doing remarkably well, he is turning out to be a polite caring young man and that is due to you. I hope that I can be there for him whenever he wants anything. I am staying very much in the background until he is ready; I hope he knows that I haven't abandoned him just because you have gone.

Seeing you today with that clinical name label on the urn brought more of the feelings. I walked round Winchester in a haze stumbled around Waterstones looking for books I'd forgotten the titles of, thought I was going mad so did the best thing, went home and pottered around the house waiting for you. Just a few short weeks ago Jenny, you and me planning the future all smiles and it was beginning to work for us, it really was. I'm sorry for going back over old ground but me really hurting and I need you now so much, please don't go.....

08:44 am 18th March

Hello, sorry about my rantings yesterday, how I feel and this morning a little calmer. Slept well last

76

night, so tired after the previous two nights. Oscar after a fun day ay Laser quest went back to Leo's for a couple of hours for games etc. Seemed to enjoy himself though didn't want to come back to our house for tea, not ready yet. Anyway, better go, got to get Leo ready for rugby and I'm waiting to hear from your Mum as to the possible trip to St. Catherine's Hill to say goodbye to you. Might see you later?

06:06 pm 18th March

How is life at the top of St. Catherine's Hill? We did by George we did it! Andy, Oscar and I climbed the slippery slopes of the hill I carrying you in a bag, holding it a little too close and I resisted calling you Little Urn, perhaps not the time and place for an Eric Morecambe style laugh? Your Mum was in the car, she knew her limitations but she was with us though not quite as in spirit as you were. Oscar led the way he knew where he wanted to say goodbye to his wonderful Mum. He told us of a tree where you had taken a photo of him with your much missed Dad when he was maybe two? He remembered, he knows of your devotion to your dad only eclipsed by the devotion you had to your son, a thirteen year old who guided your brother and little old me to the place where he wanted you to find the eternal peace that in the last months of your time with us became your major concern. We approached the tree, situated at the edge of the part of the hill by the wooden steps that descend to the peacefulness of the meadows below and, what a view! How many times did we drive past that car park with you saying this is the place where you found so much happiness and contentment? Did we stop and visit? No. I think back again to that time in The Old Vine pub a few months ago when as we sipped our early afternoon drinks and took time out from the rushing. "We don't do enough of this!" you said to me, clasping my hand amidst the revellers of that Friday lunchtime. So painfully true. Those words echoed in my subconscious as we looked across the fields and the views all around us, no rushing, and no reason to hurry just life moving on but not. As the time to say goodbye approached and the area around us seemed clear of other walkers, we felt a few drops of rain. The sun was hidden behind a cluster of grey clouds and we feared a wash out, rain stopped play? I don't think so; I looked at the sky, directly into the barrage of bullying clouds and said quietly to myself, "Jenny, do something about this, please?!" and, as we stood by the faraway tree the clouds cleared and a glint of sunlight glimpsed its way through. Time to open Little Urn. The red sweetie jar well not really, opened with the easy twist of a child eager to get hands on the goodies contained inside. There you were in a clear polythene bag!

Gone, the curves of your human form. Ashes and dust, not you, no hand to hold, no lips to kiss, no smile to melt the frozen paths of even the coldest of winter's mornings. A slight tip of the pot and out you tumbled bag intact, a rip of the top, a pull of the bag and I scattered the remains of the physical you up and down, back and forth as you fell to the ground the breeze scattering bits of you away as if spreading grow seed on unfallowed earth to bring life, the eternal gift. Oscar and Andy watched but didn't want to take turns, leaving it to me to scatter and whisper "Goodbye my love". Soon you were free drifting off in to the late morning calmness of your new home. We stood in silence for a good few minutes looking at the views our thoughts full of the happy memories of the unique you, gone but not forgotten and, as if to prove a point a family came up the wooden steps complete with collie dog who scampered by you taking time to relieve himself against the stump of the memory filled tree. We laughed knowing above the clouds you would see the funny side of a beloved dog paying due respect.

Time to go Jenny, time to go, down the steps to the pathway and a walk back along the river with promises of future picnics on sunny days, sitting by the tree thinking of you and the happy memories these will bring. From the St. Catherine's Hill of your eternity we can all sit together and remember, the smile, the laughter, the throw back of your long dark hair as you revel in us enjoying the memories of you, mother to Oscar, sister to Andy and everything to me, all of us. Rest now beautiful lady and on Mother's day.

09:28 pm 18th March

I think it's time for bed now. They say that when you have to start your life again, after a setback so to speak you look towards the "new normal". Someone somewhere came up with this phrase. However, not that I wish to rock the boat or cause consternation in the hallowed halls of the happy psychiatrists but (here we go again!) I want the normal of before."The normal of before?" I hear you cry? Yes. If you are sitting comfortably let me begin. I would be sitting here and looking at the clock waiting for a text from you. I'm ready to go, toothbrush in pocket, coat ready to put on. Beep beep "Oscar in bed, see you soon" I would leap up picking up that lonely bottle of wine itching to be opened. Open and shut the back door through the small overgrown garden. In car, start engine and the ninety second drive to your flat. I have my keys so tackle the communal door, along the short brightly lit corridor your door always unlocked, turn the handle as I do so, I hear your "hello" echoing from the lounge, the candle lit lounge. I stop in the kitchen pick up a wine glass as if that was the last thing on my mind and walk back towards you sitting in the candlelit darkness, on the sofa. I sit; open the wine, time to breathe? No, I think not, I pour, we sip, we smile, night is here the hours stretch ahead, a long time, and we have all the time in the world. We tuck ourselves up in the sensual pleasure of us and your bed, tick tock tick tock until the alarm shattering realisation that the morning has arrived, an in your face beep beep crescendo of reality. I get up and hastily make my leave giving you time to get up and get Oscar ready for school. Away from the flat I go, safe in the comfort blanket of being with you. I drive off knowing that we will be seeing each other again within hours, minutes. Oh yes it was for ever, the road ahead was there for you and me, we had time, so much time.

That was then this is now. The new normal? I'm not going anywhere tonight. The house is ready to close if I want it to. I could go out and lock the door. One slight problem, I have nowhere to go. Normal? Okay keep the new, can I have the old please? Let me know as I have all the time in the world don't I? Good night, beautiful lady.

07:00 19th March

Hello, sunny day if a little cold. How are you today? I bet the view from St. Catherine's hill is pretty spectacular. Back to work for me this morning. Hmm, this will be the first day since 2009 when I will drive off and not be in contact with you, text after text, the odd phone call and the thoughts of seeing you later. Rarely did a day go by when we didn't see each other. This is all very odd. I have to attend a back to work interview today all standard stuff but I am sure they will want to check that I'm not going Looney tunes! I'm not; just have to disguise the complete lack of interest in my poorly paid role as a Business Development Executive. Life is too short Jenny, the past few weeks have made that very clear, painfully so…. Miss you very much this morning. Speak later?

08:40 pm 19th March

Evening, busy day, brain in a scramble, don't like being back on the treadmill of the PAYE. Slowly but surely I feel myself starting to rush again. Okay I got quite a lot done today. This evening Leo and I went up to Pets at Home with the hamsters and the gerbils. At the Winnall branch they were able to take one of the hamsters but not the other or the gerbils. The Southampton branch could so we zoomed down the M3 to the branch near Shirley with Leo holding on to the hamster cage as the top had become loose. Little hammy was desperate to get out, don't think he liked the car journey! Leo kept his hand on the grill like lid to stop hammy getting the chance to explore the car! So, it was goodbye to half of the rodent collection, a little part of you in a way on the journey to a new start. I think back to those nights when I would be cooking tea and glancing out of the kitchen window I would see you in the shady lit confines of the shed up and down cleaning feeding, watering. You as always diligent and committed to what you set out to do. I miss you so much Jenny the ache whether temporarily put on the back burner by work or rodent relocating, whatever, you are always in my thoughts and the smiles that we should be experiencing as I drift to the happy memories do not materialise as I just want you here, I so want you here. I turn to look left, to look right and all I see is something to remind me of you. Then with the memory of a happy time grabbing its chance to fight its way to the surface I think of the strolls around Bath, the hushed confidences of the early part of our relationship as we, navigating our way on the snow bound M4 towards Bristol, felt at peace as you relaxed my tired eyes with needed drops of contact lenses solution, "You'll be fine" you whispered holding my hand and.. and? I drove on holding your hand. On and on we went, planning a future that was shorter than either of us then could possibly have imagined. Two years? Just two years? Why Jenny? My true soul mate in more ways than I could ever express. We could have done so much, so much. I'm not angry with you; all you had to do was to turn to me for help, turn to any of us for help. We could have done it together, the team that you so much wanted. Just ask next time and I will take your hand and guide you, our little team. You and me…. Nite.

09:48 pm 19th March

Time for bed, busy (oh how I hate that word!!) day in prospect. Will speak tomorrow evening if I don't have the chance to say hello first thing. No rushing, promise, keep things in perspective, need you close beautiful lady. Can I say that again? Need you, beautiful lady……. Xx

07:44am 20th March

Morning .Getting ready to drive to the Hilton Hotel Heathrow for a day of… just tired of it all, that feeling of rushing again, taking over so I forget the important things, can't do that really can't. Hoping you can look after me today?

09:14pm 20th March

Evening. A long day! Sorry but I did start the day angry, angry at my rushed life, angry ay being away from the opportunities to write to you, angry at you for not being here, angry at me for not being there for you on that fateful morning and just putting a stop to it all. A stop to the darkness and the illness that had taken you and beaten me. Really beaten me!

I negotiated the M3 quite well, I didn't crash the car! As I drove towards my destination to reunite me with the delights of PAYE I had thoughts, yes thoughts of just turning round at the next junction and going home. The sun had come out and I wanted to vanish into my little world and conversations with you, look at the countryside take the dogs out and the escape from the reality of you having left me with no explanation. A spur of the moment decision for you? Please say yes?! You were are and always will be everything I ever wanted so, what did I do wrong that didn't make you reach out to me for help? Do you understand what I am wrestling with? Let me know, I am here waiting...

The working day went ok, the hours dragged by to start with, I sat through the first training session keeping quiet trying to look interested, my thoughts drifted to you though I maintained a keen expression as if the Hilton Wi-Fi integration was the most important thing in my life for now for yesterday, for ever! It would have been interesting if I was asked what I was thinking about "Oh not much, just thinking of my girlfriend who recently took her own life whilst I was out working. Please, do continue!" To say that you could cut the atmosphere with a knife would be a slight understatement! Can you guide me towards salvation?

Joking aside I got through the day and even conducted the afternoon training session myself! My boss looking at me if not through me with a fixed smile on her face, asked me to do it and I did with the proviso that I could do it on my own. Standing on my own two feet in the professional world!

So I drove home knowing I can do the 9-5 for the foreseeable future. Good? It has to be for a bit, just a bit as I get myself and the future me up and running. Keep an eye on me though?

I got a letter today or rather you got a letter, from your pension provider Phoenix Life. Did you know that for just £6 a month you can take out an extensive life cover policy?! The amount of money to be paid out to loved ones for an accidental death, critical illness or even a terminal illness! Vast sums of used notes making their way to a bank account near you! What do you think? No mention of a policy involving the walk up the stairs or the closing of the bathroom door though... nite, I will resist the temptation to say sleep well...

08:20 am 21st March.

I had another dream about you last night. I couldn't find you. We hadn't been in contact all day and I was convinced that we had argued and you were in one of your moods with me. I needed to get to your Mum's house I knew you were there somewhere but found I had to crawl under a small gap in a fence to get there and into the lounge. I was desperate just desperate to find you. I was nearby in another house, people I knew in there who I wanted to avoid not for some reason wanting to talk about you. Eventually, I took the plunge and crawled under the gap and there you were sitting on the sofa curled up reading. You saw me a big smile spread across your face "Hello darling where have you been? I've been worried about you!" as you spoke you stood up and gave me a big hug and I could feel you again the warmth of your body pressed into mine one more time…. A bugger when you wake up sometimes….. Speak later, I've got quite a busy day, I will refrain from using the word rushed, you remember to tell me off if I do won't you? Love you.

08:44 pm 21st March

Funny how things creep up on you. Wherever I look these days I see newspaper reports, documentaries on TV or new books eager to deal with the important subject of depression. The illness that has blighted so many. In my twilight world of the self deluded, I can see the TV commercials popping up produced in a similar vein to those of the "Have you been involved in an accident at work?" ones that make your skin literally crawl away and hide in the furthest possible place. This is how it would go. "Are you depressed? Finding life a little tough? Does the drudgery of you day to day existences make you want to wish you were not here? Fear no more!! Thanks to our extensive research we can make things easier. Available in a weekly part work series stretching into infinity and beyond you too can learn how to beat the curse of the Black Dog, from the initial stages of feeling slightly miserable through to the final moments of booking a taxi to Beachy Head we will give you a step by step guide to your deep dark thoughts! If you subscribe today you will receive some free gifts sent to you at regular intervals, beginning with the popular game of Hangman for the depressive. Yes that's right! A game that is uniquely designed for you with a noose with a ready to fit velcro fastener!" Oh Jenny, I could go on trying to make light of a situation that I cannot reverse but in the Andover branch of Waterstones today I had a look though a book called "Under the Lemon Tree. A memoir of Depression and Recovery" Mark Rice-Oxley has written a great book on the illness that you knew and sadly embraced so well but and a big BUT here, it was too painful to read because if I knew

88

about it a month ago I would have got you to look at it, so much in the text was so familiar to what you lived with for too long! And looking through the book there is a way out apart from the obvious. No, listen, there is! Your smile, your zest, your passion, your joy de vivre could still be living and breathing and I would be still holding your hand, holding you the wonderful you, if we had the benefit of hindsight!? Bollocks? Probably! I can't reverse the one way ticket. Anyway time for bed. I am finding it a little difficult to concentrate, the noise of plenty of doors being closed after the horses have bolted… love is too small a word to describe how I feel, just one touch or……. Goodnight.

08:00 22nd March

Hello, I'm really struggling today; it's a calendar month since I've seen you. Bad night not much sleep thinking of all the things that we had planned to do together, really hurts what happened. The bed seemed really large last night, the further I stretched my arm out trying to find you, I never reached the end of the bed as if you were just out of reach. Believe me, I tried really hard. There I was last night making light of depression trying to make you smile, trying to make me smile. Not today Jenny not today.

89

The repercussions of you leaving are still causing shock waves amongst your friends. Leo is keen to take up karate with Oscar and he went along last night to see how he would like it. We picked Oscar up at 4.45 he was all ready in his gear very proud of the brown belt he got last week. Oscar was good introducing Leo to other members of the class and me for the hour, sat and chatted to your friend Maisy who co runs the class. She is still in shock Jenny and we talked about you the happy times, and your troubled times of three years ago. Maisy didn't stop saying what a kind and wonderful lady you were, no are! She seemed to know more about me and our relationship than I did! You see I still seek confirmation for myself that you really loved me Jenny. Maisy said you were so happy with me. Okay so why didn't you just say on that morning? Talking to her though therapeutic just brings all the emotions back that I failed you in some way and you couldn't trust me enough. Do you understand? I need some help here Jenny. Why didn't you just reach out and let me pull you back from the brink, stop you toppling over the edge, I was your barrier and protector. Did I fail you?

You would have been proud of your son last night, watching him in the karate class, all smiles and concentration, getting on with everyone as if he didn't have a care in the world! Leo will go next week, the last lesson before the Easter break. Oscar came back to the house to get some stuff including his karate belts collected over the years. He is so proud of them and quite rightly so. Keep an eye on him he still needs you.

Time to get on with the day. I have decided to cook a lasagne tonight. Going through the cupboards I found the beef in ale sauce that we bought. You really wanted to cook me one of your Guinness and ale pies, silly how a jar of sauce can set me off with the list of regrets and what if's that whirl around in my head like a vengeful Twister hell bent on self-destruction, not taking no for an answer, Don't worry I'll battle through Jenny I won't let this beat me. Keep an eye on me today okay? Might need a little touch or a smile to keep me going. See you then?

09:48 am 22nd March

Off to work now, I guess this time four weeks ago it was already too late? Ok then.

08:40 am 23rd March

Morning. Sorry I didn't write last night but very tired and I felt I'd given you quite a hard time, the feelings welling to the surface, if there was one person you could have relied on? So I have the nagging knocking at my soul of you not trusting enough, not trusting me enough to help you and get you back so you could live the life that you so wanted and craved for. It is a feeling of regret that I will never ever let go and as I do move on and new experiences beckon me forward your pain at the hopelessness you felt near the end will never leave me. You not being here has left this gaping chasm of emptiness, I feel as if I am only half here and that I am reaching out constantly for your presence, waiting for that elusive text the hurried phone call when you've found a bargain somewhere , the excitement in your voice. To look at you when we were on one of our trips as you visible relaxed as the stresses of Winchester faded into the background, the colour back in your face the life back in your eyes as light blocked out the darkness. Walks along the coast in Cornwall during the sunny late June of last year, discovering new places, discovering us, discovering our own Castles in the Sky on that beach near Braunton. Late night hushed conversations over a glass or three of wine and again I allowed myself or we allowed ourselves to stop rushing, your sapphire blue eyes pulling me in lead on by that dazzling smile. What a force you were to me, so much and now it's all gone and I have the memories and the photographs and kind friends constantly saying that I was the love of your life and you had found the happiness you craved. The cravings of the darkness got the better of both of us in the end and I miss you, yesterday, now and tomorrow more than my well exercised fingers pounding away on the keyboard can ever express. Despite the photographs and the memories it's all gone Jenny and I am confused and really don't know what to do…..

03:22 pm 23rd March

I think it is the hottest day of the year so far! I have just got back from a glorious bike ride pedalling as usual the length of Down Farm Lane soaking up the atmosphere of our at times breathtaking countryside. So, tell me, what is it like out walking your side? Do the fields of eternity well stretch for eternity; are there babbling brooks to cross, paths that stretch high into the clouds to negotiate? Are you out breathing in the I would imagine, clear fresh air? Does it bring you a sense of calm, the inner peace that we were always talking about? I guess you have met up with your beloved Dad again, he was always a great walker wasn't he, always rambling the heights of St. Catherine's Hill. So you, Bob with Fritz the dog? Bet it's great to see him again too, bounding towards you across the fields, tail wagging, a big slobbering kiss, the three of you walking off into the eternal dawning of a new day. Peace at last? I hope so. On that note I too feel a dog walk coming on so I'll grab my Moses staff (do send him my regards!) and yomping I will go. Speak later beautiful lady. As always, love you with well everything really. Xx

08:50 pm 23rd March

Hi there. Your Friday night going well? I have just been on the phone to Ali, over an hour we talked about you. Oh the funny stories! Ali, one of your best friends for so many years! She loved you and was so happy for us to be together but we did stumble when talking about your final days. There is no answer Jenny, no answer to the illness, dark foreboding and unrelenting in the capture of its victims. However, on a positive note, Ali and I ended our conversation with our agreement in our love for you, what type of person you were to so many people, the kindness, the time you took in caring for others and especially most importantly Oscar. Bare that in mind and the repercussions for the actions you took, we will all look after Oscar but nothing will take away the pain for us, the ones who you have left behind. No final goodbye or little wave accompanied by those looks that smile. A shame beautiful lady, such a shame. Sleep well and I hope your slapped wrists for being a naughty girl heal soon. Okay?

07:34 am 24th March

Morning, another beautifully sunny day. The weather reports say it's going to be one of the hottest days so far this year it seems if the over enthusiastic meteorologists on BBC breakfast are to be believed. They had some footage of Bournemouth beach; the summer season is being officially launched today with the use of a giant deckchair positioned strategically on the sand just by Harry Ramsden where you and I had many a battered sausage and chips sitting on the beach. I knew it wouldn't be long before a sound or image triggered a memory. We had quite a few solo trips to an always sunny Bournemouth (I've got my rose tinted spectacles on this morning) A stroll down the sharp cliff top promenade hand in hand. Ah well you know the score, to cut a long story short you and me together always together but not for long enough.

Flicking through the TV channels there isn't much on, the news is full of yesterday's Sports Relief festivities which dominated the TV scheduling last night. Everyone looked exhausted from all that running, swimming, cycling, more running, more swimming etc. Time for some comfort TV, Scooby Doo is on, also got to get ready for football, last match of the season and I am on cake duty this week so a quick trip to Tesco. With the sunny weather you and I could have been looking at the garden today, planning how we wanted it to look, something you were very keen to do! Missing you a little too much this morning. Speak later. Xx

07:48 pm 24th March

Evening. It is only early but with the spring forward of the clocks it is in what passes for my mind, 8:48pm. Also we have to be up early for a rugby tournament in Havant tomorrow so an early night is due all round.Leo is already tucked up in bed and I'm thinking of climbing that staircase soon. You remember the one, surely? Football was good. It's odd, I turned up in the park and everyone was so kind, Pam sits down to chat and over cups of tea we talk about you, Groundhog Day returns as we tread familiar ground though not coming up with a reason for what happened so I will wake and begin the whole process again tomorrow. As it was the last match of the season we all went into the club for a celebratory drink, it's never too early to have a glass of apple juice! Tee hee!! I know, I think back to the tut tuts in the Devon and Cornwall pubs as I would have just the one more! I sit outside in the blazing sunshine and some of the other parents join me, just to make sure I am okay and we talk about you. I never get tired talking about you but I'm conscious of your memory beginning to fade as time ticks on, no second chances no turning back the big and little hands to the prospect of a better future are uncompromising and unforgiving. No prisoners taken, ever. Tick tock, leading to the chimes of midnight, the witching hour in more ways than one.

At home this afternoon Oscar came round to collect a few bits and bobs. As always he was polite and well; restrained? I look into his eyes and see nothing, by that, no emotion. He is going through the motions of getting through the day. His way of coping with his Mum's departure? As if nothing has happened? Yesterday your Mum said he had got positively stroppy when he realised he didn't have gym membership anymore or that his mobile was now a pay as you go. Yes he got annoyed, he doesn't want things to change, back to normal please not the new normal! He needs watching over; you his mother need to keep this in mind. The rest of us will do our best but you are the focal point for him and always will be. You remember that, please.

Oscar flat lines and exists on the one note level. This is a dangerous place to be. To feel nothing leads to the "Why am I bothering? What is the point?" I could go on but you see the picture that can unfold? (Out of all of us you are currently the expert!) A picture that can self-paint itself on a canvas that you by your choice of actions, left for us to fill in. The possibilities are endless, the decision of a particular stroke of the brush can decide the fate of one but the echoes of that choice reverberate for an eternity that at the moment, only the person in crisis can see. I once asked you to tread softly and that sentence now resonates so as not to step on the dreams of others who have their whole life ahead of them. Repercussions, repercussions, sleep well and despite my little bit of home truth here I love you with the all that I give every day. Nite XX

07:51 am 25th March

Morning, can't talk for long have to get ready for a trip to Havant and that rugby tournament, with the clocks doing their magic of the Spring Forward I am feeling a little jaded and well just feeling rather sad this morning. Sad so sad that you are not here; it's not going away Jenny not going away in any way that feeling of just wanting to scream at you for the choice you made. I just want you here so much. Talk later. XX

10:31 am 25th March

Hello, I'm in Havant at the rugby festival. The Rugby Club positively bustling with families all sitting in their bring as you please fold up chairs, thermos flasks full of tea, the smell of freshly cooked bacon sandwiches. Small children are running around with the miniature rugby balls doing their best Johnny Wilkinson impressions charging across the newly cut grass. Everything and everyone is bathed in the warm glow of early summer sunshine, unusually warm for the time of year. You would love it. I could imagine us texting each other you happy in the garden having started working on the plans that we had to get our little patch of land ready for the summer. Your clear sapphire blue eyes looking around, scanning for little areas to make new homes for the bedding plants, not to mention the flowers which as they bloom would bring an infusion of colour to the height of summer competing with the unremitting rays of the sun. You would have been so happy, so much to look forward to, so much that we could have achieved together. But life sometimes has other plans, harsh decisions sometimes that no one can comprehend. Ah well. I am going to do the garden, well, at least try and bring some colour, it can't all be green!

Leo is enjoying the rugby, I think he has made the decision to give up the football and concentrate on rugby. He enjoys it more. There is a good positive team spirit; very character building. I can see him a few yards away from me chatting with his friends and teammates. We will have a good day. What would turn it from a good day to a brilliant day would be and I'll give you one guess, yep coming home to you, to see and touch you. A Sunday roast, a glass of red and to see you all laughter and smiles. I can dream, sometimes I feel that is all I have left.

08:08 pm 25th March

Hello sexy lady. Rugby didn't go on for as long as we expected as Leo hurt his knee and couldn't play in the last couple of matches. He was hobbling around, not faking it and upset that he couldn't continue but a bad knee restricts the movement, so we were home by 2.pm.He spent the afternoon with his Mum and I pedalled the country lanes and cooked a lasagne. Occasionally when you cooked your lasagne it was always pretty special, tenderer and softer than mine. You were a dab hand at making sure the lasagne egg pasta was just right. We would eat with garlic bread, a bowl of salad and some dressing, around the glass table in your flat. Happy times, such happy times. Everywhere I look around the house there are pictures of you, I catch the photographic stillness of your eye and, yes, and? What are you thinking? Are you trying to tell me something? Images in time preserved on glossy paper, which is all they are however, the comfort they provide is priceless. You of all people know that, the amount of photos of your father that are scattered around the house. Each day I see something different when I look at the pictures. Did I miss that sly look last time? When the photo was taken, what were you thinking? Happiness exudes and you are confident of the future that you had that we had talked about, sometimes nervously, and always positively. What am I going to do without you? I will look closely at one of the photos, a little guidance please!

Being in the house comforts me at times when things get a little dark. The only time I get a little nervous is when the time comes to go to bed. Each step I climb upwards and onwards to end another day I can't help but think that when we were together despite what was going on, everything was always all right as we pulled the covers over us and turned out the light. You would curl up and hold my hand tightly and I would let you drift off in my arms. I knew you felt safe, I wanted you to feel safe. When your fingers clasped mine that is when I felt safe as we were together and let sleep take over, into the land of dreams Jenny, into the land of dreams. Now I turn out the light and the loneliness creeps out of the dark corners. My hand reaches out to you and finds nothing and the cold of the night is often too much. Loneliness wins and I have to wait for it to bid its retreat as dawn approaches to the sound of the welcoming birdsong.

I still have to climb the stairs looking for that special place. I'm reminded of Somewhere (A

Place for Us) with thanks to Stephen Sondheim; this is for you... as always.

"There's a place for us, a time and place for us. Hold my hand and we're half way there. Hold my hand and I'll take you there. Somehow, Someday, Somewhere."

If you could give me a guiding hand tonight and for the next few thousand, I'd like that. Nite, miss you rather a lot. XX

07:17 am 26th March

Another week begins, Leo is having his breakfast and getting ready for school, I am writing a bit earlier today as I have to head off for Gatwick shortly for another day of Corporate Broadband training for a few hours. No rushing me promises! I may stay overnight haven't quite made up my mind yet, overnight bag is packed though. If I do stay then I am away from the computer so in a minute I am going to download you! Oh yes, do you fancy being downloaded and put on a memory stick?!! When you were here, I could have said that and you would have given me one of your mock shocked coy looks before saying "Mr Cook!" and I would have definitely been late for work! Oh, Jenny I do miss you...so much. Wish me luck on the M25! Speak later.

Good evening from the Gatwick Hilton! I decided to stay overnight overall as didn't finish work until nearly six o' clock, there were issues with the Broadband Wi-Fi speed and connectivity throughout the hotel that even a particularly fine strand of exemplary bullshit from me couldn't fix! I am away from home for the night for the first time since you departed and so far I am okay. I haven't been sitting here waiting for a text from you or thinking that I must send you a text so you know that everything is okay. Sure it has been a busy day and I had to do two presentations each an hour long followed by a question and answer session. For the majority of these sessions I was fine but occasionally as I was in mid flow so to speak I would come to a complete halt as thoughts of you would wash over me and that little inner voice would come a knocking, tap tap tap." Hi Russ, just to remind you, Jenny has gone, don't you remember, she walked up the stairs, and closed the door on her son, you and everything that mattered". Now, coming to a complete halt in the middle of a presentation is not necessarily a good thing. I have to grip myself from the inside without any noticeable form of movement so as not to put off or unnerve my eager students keen to learn about Wi-Fi integration. Luckily if you have a little bit of experience the pauses can be turned into the rephrasing of the previous bullet point usually to great dramatic effect if you are of a theatrical bent that is! I got away with it banishing the dark thoughts of your departure back to the land of the great unanswered question.

So, here I am sitting in the very trendy cosmopolitan bar of the Hilton Gatwick. It's getting quite busy. Two couples have just sat at the table next to me clearly meeting up for a holiday. "How wonderful to see you!" says man number one to man number two. "Are you getting better?" number one continues. Number two replies in the negative and the conversation hastily changes to the high cost of childcare, more expensive than in Scandinavia I learn. Clearly an uncomfortable conversation is avoided though woman number two has just said to woman number one that things are very up and down at the moment. Number one woman is nodding just a little too enthusiastically. Curiouser and curiouser.

Let me ask you Jenny are you able to travel freely in your new pace of eternal... eternal what? Eternal peace, eternal business, eternal Dancing on Ice? Or are you stuck in the confines of our home, your last earthly location? Can you follow me if I am away for a couple of nights? If so, can you see me in the bar area and are you tut tutting as I've just ordered another pint? If your spirit is free enough to travel, I guess you are here, maybe on one of the balconies to my left, in the plush armchair opposite me, perhaps floating around and above the tip eager bar stewards willing for them not to offer me another drink?! Good to have a little joke now and then, things have been a little bleak of late. To put your mind at rest, I am off to the room in a minute so you can forget about any more tut tutting, for this evening anyway.

In case you are interested, the holiday foursome is discussing the pros and cons of the garden shed, and the obvious concerns of the storage of tools. Time for a hasty departure. Goodnight, give me a wave, you know you want to! XX

08:20am 27th March

Morning, still at the Hilton, not a bad night's sleep the bed was huge! Reminds me of some of those beds that we had on some of our trips away. How did your night go? Another lovely day I think, trip into London for me but not for long. I haven't missed being at home, I think it was good for me to get away and take a little step back. Certainly the thought processes are a little clearer; I still at times just snatch a few sharp breaths at the thought of you not being here, especially with weather like this. Early morning and a cycle over to yours for a spicy cuppa! There you would be pottering around the flat, washing up, laundry, and the start of another day. On visits to the flat I just remember you with a positive outlook as we would sit and talk, bright eyed and full, of mischief. Off I would go to work; you waving me off into the sunshine. I do miss you. Time for a few sharp breaths I think. Speak later.

06:54pm 27th March

Evening beautiful lady. I think back to the times when we were out. Okay, we didn't go out that much socially, a couple of dinners a few pub trips with friends but I was always so proud to have you with me and I would introduce you as my significant and much better looking other half which always used to make you blush. It made you blush because you never believed it, never believed in your self or your natural beauty. When we first met you introduced yourself as "Jenny, just plain Jenny!" laughing as you said this. You were often a mass of contradictions analysing things too much, reading too much into a situation. If you hadn't done so or more realistically understood that you did this and tried to tackle it then things could have been better for you. As you often said yourself "I am a good person". You were one of the many reasons why I am or rushing up to the present moment and rapidly changing tenses was attracted to you, your kindness, your thoughtfulness, your willingness to drop everything to help someone out. At times you created a whole new set of problems, offering the helping hand of friendship and having it bitten off and spat out, as your spats with the neighbours when you were at the flat proved. I don't think I met anyone quite as unlucky as you in your choice of sparring partners at Harwood Place! You certainly hit the jackpot there but the way you handled all of the vitriol, well, I couldn't have done it! You never realised what you were capable of. I remember but a few weeks ago shortly after we had all properly moved in I saying late at night as we were curled up in bed, how much I loved you going on to say yet again that it had been true from the very first moment we met. Even then, when we were officially living together under the same roof, as if that wasn't a pretty big commitment for both of us not forgetting Oscar and Leo, you said "Ah you're just saying that it's the wine talking!" I sometimes wonder whether deep down you thought I would leave you. I know that you felt in your moments of darkness that you were a burden to me and you couldn't see what I saw in you. Silly, I pursued you so openly and for so long even surprising myself in the passion I felt for you (Love letter written and dropped through your door on that Friday

107

afternoon in January 2008, it only took us another 23 months to get together!) I don't know what else I could have done really. Perhaps with hindsight the too much rushing did take its toll, we never had enough proper time for us, I realise that now, I knew at the time but still just for us to sit back and do nothing. Just have a look at the world whilst holding hands.

The thing I miss the most? I don't say "we" anymore. Of course I can say "we" when referring to stuff Leo and I are doing and that is fantastic but saying "we" for things that we had done were doing or about to do is something that always made me step back and think how lucky I was to have you. I always felt that never doubt that.

09:47pm 27th March

I think it is time for bed soon, actually I know it is time for bed soon. Tired, very tired though have enjoyed the sunshine today. June called this evening and we talked of our guilt that we can't help feeling as we succumb to the whirlpool of emotions that has trapped all of your family and friends. We spin around desperate not to give in to the pressures of the "what if?" and drown in feelings of not being there for you at that moment. Sorry Jenny but we are all feeling this. You were so loved by so many and we want to know why you didn't just reach out.....to have

108

asked for a helping hand? Goodnight my most beautiful of ladies. I miss you... I miss you. To touch you and feel you next to me, is that too much to ask?

07:53 am 28th March

Jenny, how is the afterlife with you? In this life I slept quite badly waking at 4.am after a vivid dream of me exploring country hotels and trying to find us a good deal so we could have a couple of nights away. I found myself in a hotel very similar to the White Hart in Exeter and realised that this was the place I thought we should be. "Perfect!" I said as I strolled into the wood panelled reception area realising you would be able to get the rest and relaxation that you needed. Both of us having the time to sit and be together. You were very much still here in my little reality dream but I couldn't quite see you always being just out of reach. I so wanted to tell you about my discovery, this little hotel a rest place from everything, just for a short time. I was so happy and couldn't keep the smile off my face as I attempted to find you rushing back into the daylight and as I did so day became night and I was confronted with the darkness and the silence of our bedroom. I picked up your purple sweater and buried my head in the pillow waiting for the

dawn and the cry of the birdsong. See you later?
XX

08:59pm 28th March

Jenny, if you are looking down from your little cloud and seeing what was going on today it must have been a little difficult as we had a gorgeous day, sunshine and yep cloudless skies! You wouldn't have been able to get a comfy seat for long, if at all! Oh the levity or in your case lack of any levity at all? Sorry, but I need to laugh sometimes at the absurdity of this situation. You now reside at a peak on St. Catherine's Hill, able to view the city of Winchester and the surrounding areas for as far as the eye can see. Am I right? The freedom to do what you want must be I was about to say life enhancing but clearly I would be going down the wrong road there. Yes, the freedom to do what you want, no stress, no darkness, was it worth it?

Back to some aspect of what passes for reality I popped round to see Oscar and your Mum. Oscar had sent me a text asking in his usual very quiet way if I could bring over his Terminator Salvation DVD. I did for which he was grateful. He is so polite, reserved and dare I say it, timid? When he went off for his shower I asked your Mum how he was doing and I got the same response. "On the surface, remarkably well." I think that is the way

110

he has always been when having to put up with some of the issues he has had to face over the years. It is the Easter holidays soon and I have suggested that he may like to come out on a couple of dog walks and when Leo gets back from his holiday perhaps a day trip to Brighton? He seemed enthusiastic. I emphasise the word seemed. I leave it with you his always devoted mother.

Leo talks about you a lot; in the past weeks he would turn to me and ask a direct question. "Jenny was really ill wasn't she, there was nothing we could do Daddy was there?" He asked this same question on a regular basis every day especially in the week after the funeral as if needing some reassurance that whatever we did we couldn't have stopped the inevitable. The repercussions of your actions still reverberate like the shockwaves of a seismic earthquake. It leaves everyone on edge, in a state of disbelief, has this really happened, have our lives changed to such an extent in the blink of an eye or in your case a life ending decision that you needed to take? It is like the eternal cliff-hanger, everyone will be back tomorrow and the next day, the next month, the next year, to hopefully find out what really did happen, is there a resolution? Nite, I love you with all of me and always will forever despite the harsh moments of truth tonight. Xx

08:24am 29th March

Jenny we wake to another splendid day." Ah!" I hear you cry over your eternal breakfast, "Are things getting better Russ?" Um, no not really I was referring to the weather, the sun is blazing through the windows and the tropical March continues at least until the end of the week anyway. Each night I still wake and experience the emptiness of you not being here. This morning I am not going to go on about it, the old ground covered so thickly that I could get a job with the local council resurfacing the roads! Am off to Stratford upon Avon today for a team meeting, back tomorrow. I am sure it will do me good to "to get out and about!" as all the kindly well-wishers say. Sure there are always distractions but the dull ache of you not being here… oops I did promise no tarmacing. Speak later, please? XX

09:04am 29th March

Struggling a bit this morning, all I have to do is look at a photo of you and that word pops into my head, the word that never really goes away. Why? Time for a bike ride before Stratford. Xx

07:38am 30th March

Here I am up in Stratford Upon Avon, sorry that I didn't get round to writing last night, what with the drive up and the meeting starting a little late, I didn't really get a chance to sit down for us to have a quality chat as we were straight out to dinner to a lovely pub type restaurant right in the centre of Shakespeare's town which with the Tudor architecture bathed in the late spring evening sunshine added to the atmosphere. It was good to get together with my colleagues who are also friends to enjoy some good food and wine. I need to get dressed and showered now then breakfast before the morning meeting so will talk this evening, yes? I have a lovely picture of you in front of me. There, all smiles in the lounge at your flat sitting with Gus the dog that you were looking after at the time. Taken last year, you look as if you didn't have a care in the world. What happened? XX

08:21pm 30th March

Back home now and I want to spend some time talking over a few things with you but am really tired tonight, feel drained and need an early night. Though am in a rather calm state this evening and am able to look at pictures of you , a little smile from me and think of happy times past which are sadly where they have to remain. I will be here to talk in the morning so have your heavenly cuppa freshly boiled and we can sit down and have a heart to heart? Love you. Nite. Xx

10:29 am 31st March

Well, I was going to sit down and have a long chat with you, I'd made the cuppa, already then the phone calls and texts started coming so if you could wait until later? Got to drop Leo's bike over then a little later pop round and see you Mum as June is popping by to take Oscar out. It's all going on, let you know when I'm back. Xx

09:21pm 31st March – 08:13pm 8th April

 Hello Jenny, me back, dinner cooked, jobs done still time goes too quickly and the weekend approaches the halfway mark. It has been quite a settled day for us mortals, I'm glimpsing little moments of calm in between the inevitable regret, ifs and why? I guess you are getting used to your new life? Are you free of the pain and happy that the stroke of the blade on that morning was the way to get the peace that you so fervently sought? Did the relief seep through into your consciousness as your life-force seeped away? Was it like falling asleep to escape the exhaustion of a busy stress filled day of darkness lying ahead? Too many questions? Oh, that was another one wasn't it? Oops, one more!

Look we need to have a serious chat. I want to talk about our relationship and some of the promises we made to each other when we first got together. In those first few months the formation of a mutual bond of respect developed as we baby stepped our way forward on our own uniquely designed yellow brick road that would lead us off into the blazing sunrise of unfulfilled ambitions and opportunities. It properly began in your flat on that winter's afternoon in the early days of 2010 snow falling; the world had stopped for a precious few hours, just you and I wrapped up in each other's arms secure in the candlelight of your bedroom. I turned to you and said quietly "You realise that we are both in this for the long haul don't you?" I knew then Jenny; I knew we had just made the commitment to be together forever. In a way I had always known and it felt right to say it."Yes" you gasped "Oh yes Russ" and you at that moment emotionally relaxed, your body, lit by the candles blazing their lit shadows across the room, sunk into mine. The days rolled into one during that magical week, we talked, we laughed and just stopped and looked at us and the world around us, a pattern formed step by step on that paved road we thought would lead us to our little place, a secure home for you and me, Oscar and Leo. The foundations were in place. Brick by brick Jenny. No bad wolf was going to blow our house down. The snow remained resolute for a couple of weeks preventing the move to the new house from the old and with my old home still being packed up I would spend every night at your flat though getting up early on those white covered mornings and do the walk back to carry on packing, trudging through the snow, the Cheryl Cole song 3 Words echoing in my ears "You are the love of my life... the three words to save my life.. I love you"

Days passed and we got into the stride of 2010. I would say that we established a routine that was comfortable for both of us, gave us time to get to know each other. We began the trips away, our boys being roughly the same age, got to know each other as apart from being at school together they would inevitably spend time together at weekends. There were cinema trips and a great day out I remember riding the flumes at the leisure park in Basingstoke, you shrieking with laughter as you tumbled down the tubes into the awaiting whirlpool below.

Laughter Jenny that was the key, laughter in between the growing familiarity of what we could achieve. In those first few months we accomplished so much, the illness that had blighted you in 2009 was very much a thing of the past, holidays in Bournemouth, fun at the seaside, snakes and ice cream. Fun fun fun. We of course like any normal couple had our ups and downs including that time in the height of summer when you had written me that impassioned letter. "I hope he tells me how he feels....because I can't carry on like this." So ended your thoughts, the last few sentences suggesting that you were bottom of my list of priorities. The occasional night, the odd weekend together? Yes Jenny you were right. You see I was probably a little unsure, unsure of where we were going and when that happens I tend to back off emotionally so up front all is fine and dandy. So silly for me to behave like this! I know I fell in love with you the moment I first saw you and part of me still couldn't believe that we were together! The male complacency sets in, "Yeah this is okay and Jenny will be fine, she has her secure relationship, and it's a breeze!" I was naive to think like this, you clearly picked up on my emotional detachment. We talked, went out for the day more talking. I could have lost you again and I wasn't prepared to do that. It was entirely my fault. The long haul remember? Sorry but that jolt gave me the wake up call to realise what I had, what we had?

The summer melted into autumn and slowly with the climate change there were changes in you. The odd anxiety attack and the feelings of panic began to return. The paranoia and the odd meltdown as you would just start ranting at me, directly at me, no rhyme, and no reason. The steady fall down the cellar stairs into the darkness was beginning to which I think my darling you never really recovered. The stay at your Mum's over Christmas and I remember a happy day there as you cooked the roast Turkey. I watched you as I drank the wine!

The New Year was greeted as a march forward for us to tackle everything as a couple. We did. We spent a lot more time together in the daytimes you coming with me to work, we planned trips away, and we had trips away. You looked seriously into getting back into full time employment; you achieved that but and there is that word again, but all that time over the coming days and months you were battling with the anxiety, the dark thoughts began to return. Sleepless nights, you reaching out for me in the small hours just to make sure I was there, restless physically and emotionally.

Then that Saturday at the end of February, just after Oscar's birthday (establishing a pattern here I think) you disappeared. No reply to my texts and there I was in the gym pounding away on the cross trainer and in the reflection of the big windows I saw June getting into her bright green car with Oscar and her grandson Wilf but, where were you? Where had you gone? More texts no reply, phone calls no reply. Your car outside your flat, your home dark and empty. Home I went and then the text "I'm in hospital, I admitted myself, so sorry" You were still here, relief followed by anger, would it have been nice to let me know? On Sunday morning you called me from Melbury Lodge, I was in the centre of Winchester sitting in my car in the rain shrouded overcast car park. Your voice weak and full of regret, the restlessness of your emotions shining through. Visiting times fuck them! "No, please Russ later, I need to sleep." You slept, I waited and early evening with the rain still hogging the streets of Winchester I found you standing all forlorn looking small and lost in the reception hall of Melbury Lodge. I took your hand as I had done so many times before and we braved the weather with you wrapped up warm. We walked the windy paths of the hospital grounds and you talked slowly and quietly as the rain drops landed all around us. I held you close and told you I loved you. "Really?" a half smile and the disbelief dispelled from the muddle of the insecurities of your subconscious for a brief while. A few days passed and soon you were ready for home. I picked you up from the reception of the building full of the permanently lost souls and you came home with me. I would look after you, Oscar with your Mum. I wanted you with me, to let you sleep, to get you better. I wanted Jenny home, not the person lying on the sofa incoherent not quite sure of who I was. I wanted you Jenny, the woman who was for me in the moments of reality, my better half, one of my reasons for being me.

So you stayed you slept and on a sunny March morning I suggested you come with me to Gosport as I had some work to do down there. It was so difficult and you couldn't string a coherent sentence together the walk around the seaside resort, I almost had to guide you around, you really had no idea, no idea at all as to what was going on. We cut our trip short and drove home stopping every so often; even the car ride was too much for you. As we drove home we pulled over at the Tesco express near the house "Russ, hang on a minute, I just need to get something" you got out of the car just a brief few minutes in Tesco then home. I remember tucking you up in bed, you needed to sleep, I returned downstairs to work as you slept. You needed a deep sleep Jenny and a long sleep but I didn't realise how long a sleep you had wanted when I woke you after a couple of hours groggy and confused. I almost had to dress you saying you had to go back to your Mum's, Leo coming over, he couldn't see you like this.

Two days later I came for my customary visit to your Mum's house, there you were sitting in an ill-fitting dressing gown looking frail exhausted and lost. "Russ" you whispered holding my hand tightly "the other day in the house, I took too many pills and... and I'm so sorry if you want to go now I'll understand, please forgive me" I remember just looking at you the look of sorrow on your face. I squeezed your hand and smiled "Everything will be okay you understand, just get better, please?" I went away Jenny I went away but kept coming back. I knew I never wanted to leave you but, I was angry, angry at what you did. I wrote "While you were Sleeping" and gave it to you just to show you I cared but... it was really hard to forgive, did I ever really get over that?

You got better again and soon returned to the flat with Oscar and we established a semblance of normality, Spring turned into Summer and we went on more trips away, the highlight being our week in Devon and Cornwall. You were really on top form as we explored the West Country. Running along the beach at Braunton, snuggling up on the sand, late night drinks in the candlelit bars and discovering the delights of the numerous coastal villages that we drove through, very Doc Martin! I think that was the happiest we had been and would ever be, just for a few short days we had nothing to worry about. Boy was I in love with you; I could have stayed in that week for ever.

Back to work for you during the summer of 2011, a job demonstrating promotional products in Asda, you were so good, so organised and soon your skills were recognised. You became a temporary team leader and were interviewing potential candidates for merchandising roles

School holidays days out my sister's wedding on that scorching August weekend. "Oh she's lovely" said my cousin Kristen, "make sure you hang on to her!" Certainly, I didn't even have to answer! You charmed everyone you met rather like the first time you met my mother batting away her often pertinent questions with a smile and the skill of a seasoned politician.

Our usual routine continued. If Leo wasn't with me I would spend as many evenings as possible with you in the flat. We had many happy evenings there, I would arrive to find you in the lounge waiting for me to join you on the sofa and we would snuggle up both of us content watching a movie, the room lit by candlelight. Bliss Jenny, just bliss which on many an evening as Autumn approached set me thinking.

One morning in October, I said "Do you think we should give some thought to us moving in together?" You looked at me as if trying to access the dark recesses of my soul. "Um yes, wonderful, yes!" If you felt sceptical you had every right to. I had always been fervent in us not doing anything like this until Leo and Oscar were grown up and very much away from home! Thoughts change I wanted you also away from the flat to start a new beginning, to gain an independence in a house surrounded by friends giving you a chance to step away from the darkness that your old flat had thrust upon you, too many bad memories of the illness, too many failures from your point of view.

You were unsure, I had in the weeks leading up to your giving notice to your landlord, distanced myself from your flat, I knew this was a big change for both of us, for all four of us. I needed to explain to Leo what I wanted to do, tricky and I should have handled it better, probably buried my head in the sand to a certain extent, I distanced myself from everyone. Did I really want this? You expressed misgivings and I said to you on all days Halloween that if you were unsure, don't do it, wait until you were ready " I will still be here Jenny, the house will still be here" Thirty minutes later you sent me that text, " Notice handed in". The beginning of the end, in more ways than we could ever have realised at the time.

Did we prepare properly for the move? Probably not, no definitely not! Work was busy for me and you although you didn't tell me at the time were on the downward curve, the dark cellar steps were beckoning you down into the darkness. You asked me tentative questions "was the garage cleared out?" "The house is too small, where are we going to put everything?" I batted all the questions away and also said "no" to you wanting us plus Oscar and Leo getting together and sitting round the metaphorical table discussing the pros and cons of the move. My reasoning was that as the boys were twelve they would adapt, fit in, children are much more relaxed about these things. You didn't buy it. We didn't have the debate; this again was not what you wanted to hear, step by step down to the unlit cellar. With hindsight, I should have known better.

The day approached, I got the garage done, I cleared out the cupboards, we had room we could do it! We hired the van. It went well on that late November Friday, you and Andy thought it would be a good idea to get it all done in one day. We did, with the help of my cousin Iain with his van as well; beds, wardrobes and all, so much so that you and Oscar were able to spend the night at the house, your first night in your new home that step forward down the yellow brick road? All good, except one thing, those pills you took post move just before you left the flat for the last time, you suffering the after effects of another overdose, panic attacks vomiting and your exhausted pleadings not to go to hospital. In the flat we had found you, a note in the kitchen "No more. I'm sorry. I'm out of the way. I don't belong here. I'm sorry. I love you Oscar." A genuine cry for help or just attention seeking?

Saturday that Saturday on 26th November, you later confessed to finding the whole experience traumatic and felt that I hadn't properly pulled my weight that day as far as the house move was concerned. Possibly, yes I took an hour off to walk the dogs and spent the evening with my son oh and to help you back on your feet, literally after the overdose?! You were out of order Jenny, but I didn't realise how much a grip the illness was taking on you slowly pushing you towards that day in February. With a determination to get back to the new home you seemed better on the Sunday and we were soon sorting through stuff and enjoyed our first proper night in the house, Monday and the tension returns. I get home from work, full time job followed by audit work, we need the money and I'm trying my best. I walk in the house, "Where have you been? " I explain. As you walk off you curtly say "I didn't think you were coming back!" I cook my solo supper eat alone and we go to bed at separate times both again as far from each other as possible in bed. Fitful sleep I get up in the silence of the winters dawn. Later I see you is it you? The pain on your face, the darkness of the eyes as you sit on the sofa hands clenched together, unable to think, unable to function. We call the crisis team, Ben the counsellor you had been seeing visits wants to take the gentle approach of "let's see how it goes" the smile of the caring counsellor will remain with

125

me forever Jenny as he walks off in to the mid-afternoon winters sunshine and I watch you slip further away from daylight to darkness. I help you to pack your bags and I drive you and Oscar who had just back from school over to your Mum. I have to drive to Manchester you need to be with someone, you can't be on your own.

Over the next few weeks, life takes begins to set its own pattern, you stay at your Mum's, I visit I take you out for little trips, you spend time at the house with me, your medication is increased and communication becomes increasingly difficult, your short term memory is gone and as each day passes you withdraw from life. I begin to feel the strain myself wondering if the decision for us to move in together was the right one. Can we survive this? As the days in December arrived the pressure really began to take its toll, culminating on a Monday morning just as I was about to leave for a day's work in Brighton. Yes, you and Oscar had moved back on the Saturday night, I had suggested it "Yes, let's do it!" pinged your positive text into my mobile inbox.

Back you and Oscar come and Saturday night we stay up late talking, determined despite our separate misgivings, to make this work. I am out all day Sunday with friends in London, you seem okay when I leave, I remember being tense on the drive talking to friends as we whizz up the M3, I grip the steering wheel too tightly, I drive too fast to relieve the pressure. Home mid- evening, I find you sitting just sitting very quietly. How do I know things are not right? For a start no washing up done, clothes hanging out of the linen basket. The Jenny I know wasn't sitting in the lounge that evening. "I need sleep, really need to sleep, do you mind if I go to bed early?" you go; I watch you go walking slowly, step by step as if negotiating an insurmountable journey. Later I come to bed you are restless and sense you are awake but don't say anything. I reach out for your hand, you grip tightly.

You grip my hand tightly the next morning.Oscar is off at school you go upstairs, "Jenny, are you okay?" Silence. I find you in the bedroom, just standing there shaking your head kneading your hands. Hand in hand we walk downstairs you sit on the sofa, I call the crisis team, they agree to visit. Ben arrives accompanied by a colleague Paula. I make cups of tea all false smiles and from the kitchen as I listen to Ben and Paula talk soothingly to you, yes you Jenny, trying to get through the unyielding barriers of the deep depression, words and phrases such as the counselling metaphorical comfort box that contains hot chocolate, Harry Enfield DVDs speak themselves into the atmosphere. I walk back round, you are twitching almost shaking surrounded by the smiles of the ignorant and ill prepared. The conclusion from Ben and Paula was that Jenny would be perfectly okay to be left in the house for the few hours until Oscar got back from school. "Yes Russell she will be fine!" they reiterated as I walked them to the car. I told them about having read the recent headline grabbing story of the father who begged for his depressive daughter not to be released from hospital. She was, she jumped off a building a couple of days later. "Ah" smiled Ben you only read about the unsuccessful cases not the successful ones!" I look directly at the two of them "I was talking from the father's point of view". The fixed smiles from the so called experts say it all. Despite promises to the contrary Ben and his team never called me again. Clearly I was trouble Jenny; I dared to have an opinion about your welfare!

When I get back in you are sitting on the sofa. Your eyes are black with deep fear. I go for the truth "If I'm right and I go out leaving you on your own for a few hours and these feelings get worse you won't be able to cope and in a moment of desperation you will want to end the pain?" "Yes, yes I know" you say. "If you make that decision" I continue "the first person to find you will be your son, you do realise that?" Then Jenny if you can remember the tears begin to fall, cascading down your cheeks, you are shaking with emotional pain and fear. You really had no idea, it hadn't occurred to you until I pointed it out. Your son, the most important component of your life encounters a scene that will change his life forever. No doubt, no question, an end to your life creates a life changing experience? Within minutes I get you dressed and we drive to your Mum's. She is out and on this crisp winter's day we walk or rather I walk you around the park, I holding your frail figure tightly it is as if you have aged 20 years. Oh Jenny just to look at you that day as I made you see the fields and the beauty of the scenery that surrounds. Nothing from you, we see Ellie and the dogs walking towards us I insist we say hello. "Oh please Russ no!" Yes Jenny yes, Olivia runs towards you wagging her tale. She brushes against you nearly knocking you over. You manage half a conversation as we exchange pleasantries but none of us hang around for long.

So Jenny, to your Mum's she accepts the situation straight away, she has been through it so many times, the school is called with instructions for Oscar to make his way to his Gran's house and I leave for Brighton this time without you. Whenever we went don't you remember, it was always sunny? As I make my way there the clouds thicken and darken and by the time I arrive it is cold bleak and the rain soon descends, a reflection on how we were all feeling? I think so. That evening I pack clothes for you and Oscar, your Mum's for the foreseeable future.

In the lead up to Christmas I am busy with work, I visit you every day and at times behind the blankness of your looks and the darkness of your eyes I see glimmers of the woman I fell in love with, a spark that isn't yet strong enough to light that flame though.

We are in constant touch by text and sometimes I wonder how to handle you, handle this? Do I take the kid gloves "there there" approach or perhaps a little tough love? One morning this decision is made for me by you! I am just about to leave for work and you send me a text asking if I could drop a DVD over for Oscar. I duly do, we chat, and you are on your own. You then mention that Oscar has a youth club cinema trip planned and will need 3D glasses. You smiled at me so sweetly as I asked quite curtly why you didn't let me know before I left the house. "Oh well I'm not really with it, very whoozy!" I drive off and get the glasses and on getting back standing in the doorway I lose my temper, the pressure has built up. Each time I had visited you had always asked if us moving in is what I had wanted, throwing everything back for me to mentally churn over, well enough was enough! Passing you the glasses I speak " If you keep saying to me every time I come round if I want to be with you, eventually I am going to start to actually question what you say, it is going to eat away at me until I come round to what you keep questioning within yourself. When this happens all that I feel for you will be emotionally transferred into feelings of pity, I will be caring for you as if you were an elderly relative. When this happens and I stop thinking about you as a woman and my partner, my lover whatever, we are finished. Do you understand? We are finished; have a serious think because even though you are ill you have to take some responsibility for your recovery as at the moment we have flat lined, there is nothing for us to cling on to." Off I go to work leaving you with that thought and we didn't see each other for two days. A long two days eh? Tough love, did it work? I don't know by this time despite moments of light, the darkness of the long fall down the cellar steps was becoming increasingly difficult for us to banish.

The week up to Christmas, me busy with work, to Exeter for a team meeting, we are in touch by text, you are more positive, I spend an afternoon in our favourite city Christmas shopping, get you some pressies! Home not feeling well and the build up to Christmas is blighted by me going down with a nasty bug to which ends my planned visit to you on Christmas Day, cancelled. I can't get out of bed, caught a bug, a virus? Maybe but looking back on it Jenny I was just exhausted, I'd trod carefully over a no man's land of unexploded eggshells and the strain was getting to me, yes me, Mr Invincible, your Knight in shining armour was in need of a polish! We saw each other briefly on Christmas Day evening but not again until the 27th when I arranged a cinema trip to see "Arthur Christmas" I thought it would do you good, a life enhancing film which Leo, Oscar and I had seen, but not you so armed with 3D glasses and bags of sweets off we drove to the Basingstoke retail park. You loved the film and for the rest of the day you were Jenny, the Jenny I fell in love with, laughing, joking, eating the Roast Turkey that we had cooked together, playing Wii games with the boys, interacting, taking part in life again. Was this day just an exception to the rule of the depressive illness? I feared it was as the very next day when I met you at your Mum's the anxiety had returned, you and I navigated the aisles of Sainsbury's, you held my hand, I held you close, just to give you the reassurance.

With the beginnings of 2012 looming rather large on the horizon we did need to address our domestic situation. Time for a few tentative nights for you and Oscar to spend in your new home, our new home? We decided to give it a go so on the day before New Year's Eve and you both came over, and we began our long delayed new life together. It needed so much work, the juggling of a small house making it habitable for at times four people. We worked hard in the daytimes, rearranging furniture, and storing boxes of belongings in the loft and concentrating especially on getting Leo and Oscar's room comfortable and welcoming for them. Big changes for you and me but even bigger for the boys. Over the next few days your mood perked up as you took an active role into changing a house into a home, I worked to your designs and was so pleased to see in the days leading up to me going back to work your mind being occupied with positive thoughts. You got Andy putting up shelves; we changed over washing machines, set up the Sky HD. Our house became a home and feelings of domesticity took centre stage as we cooked together, ate together, we were together Jenny the family unit that you so wanted was almost in place! We were moving on from the baby steps, the steps became strides and we walked into the lights of the new January dawns until just a few days into our new life...

It coincided with my return to work. Something happened. Was it being alone in the house? As my first day progressed with admin work to be achieved at home I slowly watched you fall apart, you said again you needed sleep and I checked on you every so often and just sat and looked at you asleep, eyes crunched up in pain. Oh my dear Jenny what was I to do? What was I to do? A day or so later you stand in the lounge all confused "I'm not doing well Russ, I feel everything is closing in, please help me, please". If I was out you would send the text "I love you Russ, I'm scared". That said more than anything.

The days go on I take you to your Mum's for the daytimes so you can get looked after. I take you for a meeting with Ben and the focus is on your tension, a seeming unwillingness to cooperate. Suggestions are made for you to help yourself "I'm not well, I can't" is all you say. I sense Ben's frustration and mention to you that Ben might have a point.

Later as we see out the last few hours of the day the tension in the house is palpable. We had been through the motions, dinner, Oscar at Youth club, Leo and I watching Peter Kay's latest DVD. You sit in silence then when the boys sleep you turn on me. Why had I sided with Ben, two men ganging up on a defenceless woman? Why had I not done this, done that, your eyes as you spoke dark and angry, almost spitting at me. "You don't want me here!" I lose my temper, all the frustrations well up and I just look at you incredulously as you get angry at me for wearing my slippers in the garden, gosh, I could get dirt in the bed! No Jenny this has gone too far we pass Saturday in restrained silence. I am lost trying to find you behind the darkness. Sunday a lifeline and we have a late roast with Iain and Molly at their house, Oscar and Leo play Nintendo's we eat, and you are quiet and talk to Molly for a long while. As we leave Molly pulls me to one side "She is very very ill". Sunday evening Jenny we argue again when I gently ask you what you will be doing on Monday. Your dark eyes burn into my soul "Why don't you think I will be able to cope!?" That night our bed becomes a lonely place.

Jenny the funny thing is often after one of our late night rows you didn't seem to remember anything the following morning. I got the impression that as the days progressed you came to rely on my support, my love more and more as if you had given up on yourself, you had to take my hand and let me guide you, advise you. A change in medication and your moods pick up, we have days out in Cardiff and Bath, you start to smile again and then one morning after the alarm has gone off for the 7.am start up you come bounding downstairs and jump onto my lap as I sit on the sofa working. You give me a big hug and kiss saying "You know I really think this is going to work!" and over the next couple of weeks, the smiles return, the tiredness recedes from your eyes and we start to see the pathway forward, all four of us begin to establish a routine, a relaxed routine and I am with Jenny again, the Jenny I met in the school playground in 2006. I hold your hand in love not support. We have a great weekend, visits from June, Wilf and Ali; you are in your element, mistress of the house with the kettle permanently boiling!

The determination you feel in wanting to get better and be you again set you on a path where there really was no turning back. You call me one day from a garage near Fair Oak, you have bought a new car, traded in the old one, later you talk to me about returning to work, setting up a date towards the middle of February, probably after half term? You bolster me on and support me as I struggle with the stress of what we have been through, work is getting harder, this time I'm not sleeping, I go for blood tests you hold my hand this time as I return from the early morning appointment at the pathology lab. "It will be fine Russ, do phone up and get the results, we don't want anything happening to you!" you imply that me not being here say if the stress took its physical toll was not an option that you wanted to consider…..

The fun continues I get up to cook the breakfast omelettes for the boys most mornings. One day you came bustling down and started moving in front of me then behind me putting away last night's washing up. "Am I in your way?" you say with just a passing interest. "Yes" I say going on to explain that I can't cook in such a small kitchen with you walking about, give me a couple of minutes please! With a huff and a puff you don't blow the house down but walk off and have a sulk with me for a half hour, then it is all forgotten. What a relief you must be getting better! A little normality, Jenny you are getting better!

So much better in fact that when I return from a two day working trip to Watford I discover a new addition to the family. We had discussed getting a dog, you and Oscar were really keen and I thought the idea good in principal but Jenny let's see how you are, get better first, see how the return to work goes? Well you completely ignored all my suggestions and in fairness I wasn't at my most gracious when I walked in that evening "What the hell is that?" were the first words that left my lips that cold winters late January evening. However it became clear to me that the dog made you happy, you had something to focus on, training the little dachshund cross, Heinz, you and Oscar had decided on a name, soon to be renamed Billy Heinz, the Billy after your father you said. For the first few days all was fine though you failed to understand how young Billy couldn't let you know when he was about to have a wee on the carpet. A widdle later and you would march over to him pointing an accusing finger "Outside!" as you picked him up and showed him the back garden. Time and again you did this to no affect.

Billy Heinz became part of the extended family, he came with us on two trips to Poole, we walked him in Poole Park, and Oscar took him for a ride on the train. All happy in Jenny's world as you charged round Poole market on a frosty winters afternoon picking up goodies for the dog, full of the joys Jenny until a few days later as we are driving to Brighton. "Are you okay?" I say taking my eyes off the road for a couple of seconds as we zoom down the M27. "Yes, yes, just feeling a little under the weather, I'll be fine", you look thoughtful, anxious, could it be the lack of sleep due to the dog? Billy was yelping quite a lot at night, keeping us awake, more so you and you needed your sleep, always did.

The February days began to form a familiar pattern, I would go to work your day involved with more work around the house but every evening as we approached Valentine's Day you are going to bed earlier, your eyes are looking tired, you almost plead with me one night to let you know if I can see the signs of the depression coming on. I wait for the right moment, sorry Jenny perhaps I should have said something earlier but I waited,

waited to that weekend morning when you said the same thing to me three times over in a half hour period. "That's the third time you've told me that today Jenny!" Always one of the signs for you, the signs of the cellar door opening my lovely. Sorry, so sorry. You looked at me mouthing "no!" as you took a step backwards across the lounge. It was if I had lit a fuse, slowly the anxiety returned, you looked to me each day for guidance, in the evenings wrapping yourself around me on the sofa wanting to be safe a break from the darkness. In those ten days leading up to the Thursday morning things were getting a little tricky, not just for you but for me work wise. I was under pressure I was underperforming, too much juggling Jenny, too much juggling. So a few days concentrating on work and I took my eyes off you for a little while, only for a little while, but….

Valentine's Day and pressies cuddly dog big card, we exchanged gifts but that night I did sense the clouds forming, half term which kept you occupied was in mid swing and you went out with Oscar, and Heinz, took the little dog round to see friends, this cheered you up a bit. We talked in the evening about how difficult you were finding it with Oscar, he was answering you back, and you felt powerless. Then the self-doubt crept in about getting the car, should you have done it, conscious of not being fit enough to go back to work, to earn the money then the guilt about the dog, you felt it wasn't working, why wasn't the puppy adapting? "I can't do this Russ, I feel helpless". The things you had set into motion as a way out for your depression as a way forward for your recovery had as far as you were concerned turned on you and added to this sense of failure. You had let yourself down you thought and felt a burden to me as the guilt crept in thinking of me looking after the dog in the early hours as you slept.

Oh Jenny what a mess as your final weekend approached. You put on such a brave face but the anxiety increased, the cellar door was unlocked and the unlit stairs beckoned you closer, each day, closer.

Slowly the depression is strangling you and you whisper to me on the Monday evening "I am trying to keep it together for Tuesday", Oscar's birthday. Monday had not been a good day, you book an appointment with the crisis team, Kathy and Clive take you and also take care of little Billy, I get home to find no dog, you explain that temporarily he is to stay with them just to take the stress away until you get better. I ask about your visit to the hospital. Rather blankly you say that they have increased your medication, an extra sedative, no counselling or anything, from your point of view absolutely no support from the professional body that should be helping you.

Oscar's birthday, we order some things for him online, you and he go to a Toby Carvery, his favourite, Leo and I can't make it but I promise you we will celebrate at the weekend. You agree. You do keep it together and you make it a memorable day for your son as he takes on the life of a teenager.

Work so busy I am out early morning and not back until mid-evening, you cook tea each day and on the Wednesday we have a lovely chicken korma at my suggestion. We sit down and watch a movie, you are tense, almost statue like as the film unfolds. As we tidy up after dinner you grab my hand and pull me towards you a hug and a kiss "Thank you for looking after me" I think no more about it, later in bed we curl up in each other's arms, you relax a bit and we go to sleep.

Thursday 23rd February. 7.05 am. You have just got up wearing your grey dressing gown drinking the cup of tea I made you. I sense your anxiety. I look you in the eye "Listen if you need anything today; let me know, phone or text me okay?" You nod "Oh, could you put the bin out?" "Which one?" The ordinary one thanks!" I rush off up the drive not looking back to say goodbye, I am late, important not to be late....

The next time I see you mid-evening as you lay in the lounge eyes closed, and in the first few hours of your eternal sleep, you look pained, troubled, your taxi is waiting outside to take you on the first part of your final journey. I think Never Again. So much to say....

Jenny, I started out writing this part on 31st March to try and make sense of our relationship but as the words flowed it became clear as I thought and read back that the inevitable ending to your journey and our story was set in motion, that day I visited you in Membury Lodge back in February 2011. That is why the focus is on the last three months (not intentionally when I started writing this last entry) when with what benefit hindsight can offer me I have traced the pattern of your decline to lead up to that February 2012 morning. I needed to write it out and offer to you my perception of your last year. You didn't recover; you did your best the illness progressively took hold. You fought so hard. We had moments of steadiness but the lows overtook the calm times, it became increasingly difficult as we progressed sadly so sadly towards the conclusion that you reached to end the pain, a conclusion that we had saved you from before. I wanted I still want to get angry with you, angry for you leaving me, angry for you not trusting me enough to save you, angry at you leaving your son to question so much about you and how you could do this. I am angry so angry so fed up, so frustrated so hopelessly in love with you that my life has stopped. I am tired and just want you here despite the difficulties and exhaustion of the last few months. And, those weeks were difficult and for the majority of the time unhappy, very unhappy, a life for all of us that had run out of ideas and direction. I see now that you did what you had to do, you had given up; the pain was too much. However the choice you made has changed so much and each day I am on a constant search for the good in this. What do I have to overcome to start the recovery, to get through the need to have you here, to look into your eyes, to see you laugh, to see you smile and to once more lose myself in the warmth of your body and feel at one with you and at peace with the world? If you have any ideas?!! As a conclusion, we knew when we finally got together, that we would be in it for the long haul. The letter that accompanied the iPod you bought me in the summer of 2010 began "You and I are in this together..." So Jenny, what changed? I remember back in that blissful snow filled New Year many many days ago when we finally walked along as a couple I hated it when you left, I never wanted to be apart from you I felt that whenever I saw you walking towards me that I was home. I liked being at home.

It is now 8.13pm on 8th April and tomorrow I will update you on the events of this week. Have you been watching and reading? If you are keeping an eye on us from your little Cloud nine even you may realise that it might not be the place to rest this Easter weekend? Nite. Xx

08:57pm 10th April

Happy birthday! Forty seven, if you had still been around of course. So, has it been a busy week? Yes and no, we've had the Easter Bank holiday weekend and I've been staying at Leo's Mum's looking after the dogs, cats and assorted fish whilst they are all away. Yes I know, you were never keen on me staying at my old house, interacting with my old life but you are not here anymore so you don't really have a leg to stand on. Sorry you don't do you?! Hopefully there isn't a sense of humour bypass your side? Actually, there is quite a bit for us to have a chat about but am very tired, I am driving to Cardiff tomorrow night, we will talk when we get to the hotel, okay? Have a good rest of your birthday; continue to sleep well sexy lady. Xx

08:09am 12th April

Morning from the Hilton Cardiff. Sorry for not having written last night. Wednesday proved to be a little hectic, no I wasn't rushing around just getting on with day to day life. Training at the Hilton Basingstoke which took up the majority of the daytime plus the early morning river walk with the dogs and the afternoon walk with the dogs! Actually they are looking a little jaded, perhaps three walks a day is a little tiring. They didn't get a third walk yesterday evening as it was raining and I needed to set off for Cardiff at a reasonable time. The drive was fine, the first time I have been up that stretch of the M4 since you left. As I passed the junctions to Bath and Bristol, I thought of our happy times West Country way. Anyway, you would love this hotel, a King Size bed so large that it must be for a morbidly obese monarch. And the state sized bathroom. You would have been in there for ages pottering about! I remember the days when I used to send you photos of the various hotels I was staying in when you weren't with me and your funny jealous texts back! Ho hum, what's done is done. Better get on, breakfast plus work before the drive home. Don't want to be caught rushing do I? Will speak properly later ok?

10:30am 14th April

Hello! It's been two days; over two days since we last spoke! I feel that I have neglected you leaving you to float around in the afterlife adrift in the astral plains? Am sure you are having fun, is the contentment and peace making itself known as you adapt to a more settled existence? I hope so, really hope so.

"What has been going on down on jolly old Earth then?" I hear you crying out. Oh, where to begin, when did we last speak before I embarked on my analysis of our relationship? Okay it's not as if that much has being going on, I could wax lyrical about all the wild parties that I've been to, the laugh a minute pub crawls around Winchester. What a time!! Yeah I know I wouldn't have done that if you were still here let alone now. Give me a long dog walk through the willowy grassed Easton Field and a stroll along the river and I'm happy. Perhaps the odd glass of fruity red to seal a good day, you and me after a glass or three of fruity red eh?

I enjoyed my week animal sitting. The dogs, cats and assorted fish all got on well, three dog walks a day and time to relax and think and as you know a retrospective of our relationship and what you meant to me and what you mean to me now. What do you mean to me now Jenny? I still feel abandoned as if you bailed out just when the plans that we had rather haphazardly put into place were beginning to take shape. Like a newly seeded patch of earth we were waiting after much cultivating and tending, for the right amount of sunlight to guide us forward, take those steps to a better place. Such a shame Jenny and the one regret that I will always have whatever happens to me in the future will be the feeling of "there was so much more to do, we could have done so much" I hope you understand what you've given up young lady...

Talking of things that you've given up, Oscar is doing really well. The other weekend your son, Leo and I drove to Lyndhurst for the clichéd walk in the country. I made the mistake of letting them go to the shops on their own in search of goodies! When I say goodies I thought perhaps an overpriced trinket celebrating the countryside spirit of Hampshire but no, when I met up with them on the high street they walked towards me armed with an array of hiking/walking sticks that would have the likes of Ranulph Fiennes, Bear Grylls and other feted explorers passing out with envy. "How much?" I asked, "Oh, only £57!" they uttered in unison. I see, two boys with more money than us then? No matter, we met up with Iain and Molly for a two hour walk through the New Forest so hiking sticks put to good use! The sun shone down on us and it was a relaxing afternoon, the highlight being the drive home as the three of us talked about you, funny stories about you which had us all laughing and that has to be a positive thing. You are missing out on so much…. And that night you missed out on a lovely Roast Chicken, so there!

Waking on the 10th April your birthday was a tough one! All your close friends were in touch with either me, Oscar, Andy and Belinda. Kathy got in contact wanting to know the location of your tree at the top of St. Catherine's Hill. So mid-afternoon I met up with her Clive, Sheila and young Heinz and up the wooden staircase we climbed talk of you, thoughts of you and the obvious painful talk of your final days and the disbelief of you not being with us. To the tree and part of your earthly ashes are still on the grass track, resolutely refusing to leave eh? We did wonder if you had anything to do with the weather that day as in the space of a half hour we had, blinding sunshine, torrential rain and two bouts of hail, the first stone sized pellets fell at the foot of the tree. On the walk down the muddy slopes we got hit by mini shards of ice coming straight out of the low cloud cover and apart from being rather painful, nearly knocked us over into the emptiness of fresh air and open space that would have carried us rather quickly to the bottom of the hill. We could have met up again, sooner than any of us had planned! I am sure you can see the funny side.

Oscar is with Leo, Ellie and Doug, he went over yesterday afternoon, and it is good to see him smiling and relaxed and having fun not just with Leo who is being brilliant with him. He is just enjoying being with his friends and dare I say it, learning to be a kid again? You would be so proud of him and he still misses you so much, he has posted more fun pictures of you on Facebook of "his wonderful mother". You were and still are. Speak later sexy woman, miss you.

08:16am 15th April

Morning on a cold chilly but Spring like day. Another weekend half way through, time goes too quickly, starting to get very conscious of that Jenny, very conscious. When you left I was resolute in my determination to move forward very quickly, get out of the rut all change push forward zooming through the stations of life, my own little intercity express making good time but not rushing. Funny how the routine of getting through a day can take over and ambitions slip to second place not deliberately I hasten to add but the day to day aspects of life pull you forward slowly but surely. All of a sudden, there I am on the sidings, the secondary track, chugging along, bogged down by routine, stopping at all the secondary stations. I watch that express service zoom by, the main track sparkling with electrical energy, ambition now being driven by others as I am reduced to shovelling coal into the never satisfied furnace. Watch it burn Jenny, and within minutes all that effort has disappeared in puffs of smoke that disperse into the sky. I woke this morning with an intense feeling of your physicality, I could hear your voice in my head as if you were yelling at me to move back onto the main track, " Get back on board Russ, you're slipping, don't let that feeling go, please!?" Okay, I need to refocus and banish those old habits that creep up when they are least expected. So easy believe me so very easy.

Oscar and Leo were together all day yesterday and had a great time. Your son is now the proud owner of a new bike; he along with Ellie and Leo went to Hargroves and chose one which Ellie paid for and the look of joy on your son's face Jenny, a look of release as if he had been let out of prison," I can cycle to St. Catherines Hill, and I can...." Endless possibilities Jenny, all for the good. So much laughter yesterday, our sons were here for dinner, plenty of pizza and games of Super Smash Bros Brawl. I drove your very happy and chatty son home at 9.pm. Your Mum was pleased of her restful couple of days and also pleased for her grandson looking happy as if he was embracing life, taking steps forward with happy memories of you by his side. Time for another cuppa, speak later and thanks for the little wake up call this morning, we don't have all the time in the world do we, you know that more than anyone?

08:19 am 16th April

Another week begins and I'm getting myself ready for an exciting day in the big city. Shouldn't be too bad as the sun is out, melting away the overnight frost. Here we are in April with little snippets of winter weather! Sunday proved to be a happy day, Leo went off cycling with friends, and I went off cycling along the country lanes and into Winchester to follow the usual routine of picking up the Sunday papers. Iain came over and we went for a walk. To the right of the house we strolled and under the railway bridge to a country lane that after twenty minutes brought us out at the top of the village just by the village vet's vast estate, animals everywhere all brought to focus by the barking dogs. I've lived in this village for thirteen years and have never done that walk before. Each day is a new adventure eh?

As we strolled the chicken roasted in the oven, roast potatoes nestling comfortably on the shelf below sizzling in goose fat. Later when Leo and

151

Oscar joined us the four of us tucked into a feast watching episodes of Futurama. So a happy day all round, Oscar back to your Mum's early as it is Back to School tomorrow, Iain drove him back on his way home.Leo got on with his homework before his bedtime. Just before, we watched some old Morecambe and Wise sketches. He is old enough to appreciate the humour now, laughing away at the breakfast striptease routine. Like father like son. Then bedtime, a restless night for me. I woke at 2.am feeling very panicky again lying there for a while trying to work out the reasons why. I think it's the loss and feelings of loneliness seeping their way into my bones. You see, on paper, Sunday was a good day but looking back to that time just a few hours ago I recognise what was wrong what still is wrong and will be for a little while to come. I feel I am only half here, going through the motions as if trying to create a perfect scene of domesticity almost Truman Show style. I'm a bit player putting on a show, wearing a mask, wishing I was fully participating as part of a couple. Wherever I look in the house there is a photo of you, smiling out at me, saying "Hello!" from a past time that I can't reach. Do you understand where I am coming from? I still am unable to process you not being here. If I was a fictional character say a Vulcan from Star Trek the phrase would be "That is illogical". How do I find the logic Jenny? What path do I have to tread? See you later. Xxx

08:15am 17th April

Here is an interesting fact for you. My Great Aunt Molly lived in a little terraced house in Sturminster Newton. She used to own a wool shop and whether she made her fortune from sales to the knit and pearl brigade is unclear but she had enough money to retire to the sleepy Dorset village in the 1960's. We always used to visit her about twice a year in the 1970s often on Boxing Day for her home made mince pies I remember. She also used to have a rather wonderful garden the centrepiece being a plum tree that used to produce the goods every summer! And the point being? Well, Molly in the last few years of her life suffered a form of Alzheimer's which gave her an extraordinary recall for her early life as a child in post Victorian England but she couldn't remember what she had done that morning! She went through the days in a state of deliriously happy dottiness keeping old newspapers and copies of the Radio Times from years previously and often reading them as if they were the up to date editions. Thirty two years ago she died. My father was staying with her at the time, he'd taken his eighty one year old Aunt an early morning cup of tea, she thanked him as she sat in bed drank the tea put the cup down and passed away, left the planet, caught the Celestial Express. What a way to go! I remember telling you this story after Iain, Leo and I made the pilgrimage to her house last summer. You thought that would be rather a nice way to begin the eternal journey…. Get my point?

Thought I would relate that tale to break the ice on this rain covered overcast morning. I had a bad day yesterday most of the time I was exceedingly angry with you so very cross at what you did not just most importantly your son, but to me, my son, your Mum, brother, not to mention assorted family and friends. Temper these feelings as the anger is replaced by such a deep longing to see you again, I missed you more yesterday than anytime since you left. So anger leads to frustration at not being able to talk to you!

Of course even though I try to put things into perspective I am walking around with a pair of rose tinted glasses permanently attached to my face. I can't focus on what was real when you were here, the tension and unhappiness as you battled the illness and the psychological effects of what that did to you and me! The thoughts I had of whether we could survive together would our relationship survive, would you ever be able to see the light of life again? Thoughts that are hard to bring to the surface. A miserable future for a lot of the time was on the cards. Sorry Jenny but now you are free of the pain can you see the pain that was here all around when you were here next to me? These thoughts are soon banished. All I do focus on is those west country beach walks, the "first date" cinema trip or the time in the summer of 2009 shortly before we got together when you and I stood in my kitchen washing up the plates after our roast beef supper, we stood side by side, gently touching, little glances, half smiles as we began our journey….. No bad thing? Not sure sometimes.

07:57 am 18ᵗʰ April

Another wet and overcast day although there have been some flashes of early morning sunshine. Yesterday was a lot better thought wise. I spent the time at home and got on with trying to move forward, progress things, looking for better paid jobs, registering with voice over agencies, contacting publishing companies to discuss ideas for features. Just for a little while I can focus on trying to wade my way effectively out of the psychological quicksand that I find myself sinking into most of the time. I can't dismiss the feelings of wanting you back and those thoughts are foremost in my mind at the moment but I can find a way to sideline them. I still want to ask your opinions on things, have a cuppa, have a cuddle, and know that everything will be all right because you are at my side. It's hard,very hard, I miss you so much but perspectives must be sought.

I had a good evening with Leo last night, I met him at his Mum's house after the dog walk and we got home and made a scrummy shepherds pie before watching some Two Ronnies sketches (No fork handles, handles for forks!!). A much happier evening than Monday when I was fractious and withdrawn, I just let him watch TV as I moped about. Not good. The selfishness of grief takes away the realisations that others will be suffering too and coming to terms with life without you. As I've said before, Leo talks about you a lot as he gets to grips with what you did. It's affected him so much and I have been dismissive of his feelings thinking he is doing okay. On the outside yes so I am trying to put my emotional egotism aside and make it better for him and create some semblance of normality. Right off to work, better pull my socks up and try and earn a living! Off to Cobham for more Hilton Wi-Fi training. Take care and have a happy day floating about. Keep an eye on me okay? XX

07:31 am 19th April

Guess what? Today is an anniversary of sorts. Have a think, see if you can remember! Will let you know shortly once Leo is off to school.

Have you worked it out yet? Well, 2006 it was, in the local primary school playground and I got chatting to "a lady called Jenny who is mother to Oscar, a friend of Leo's; dark haired, attractive with glasses, how can I put this.... I think we clicked, both single.... We talked and talked as we strolled down the road towards the local Tesco. I was walking her home." The journal entry goes on and we ended our meeting very formally with a shake of the hands with you smiling at me "It's Jenny, plain Jenny!" "I don't think so" I thought to myself as we exchanged numbers with you brushing your hair back saying "Nice to talk to you Russell" Off you walked with me watching you go and for various reasons which we talked about endlessly in the future, we didn't speak again until October 2007! What a waste of time don't you think? Funny, I think back to that time and the first proper time I spoke to you although I had seen you about before with one particular memory from about 2004 and I was cycling very fast past the village pub. I saw you, you in long blue coat, short bobbed black hair just smiling standing outside the post office with a large dog, certainly your Fritz. I remember almost stopping and staring thinking "What a beautiful lady!" I never stopped thinking that and never will. Who would have thought Jenny from that first memory that I have of you how things would pan out? From that first meeting to nearly six years later and the last when I am standing in my living room on the evening of 23rd February and there you are eternally asleep in front of me on the floor, all ready to go, gone for ever…. Happy anniversary. Xx

04:59pm 21st April

The hail is pelting down all around I can hear it tumbling off the roof sliding down onto the ground like someone emptying shale slowly down a drainpipe. I had just been thinking of going out for a cycle, so will wait a bit and have a chat with you. Saturday, good old Saturday. It's been a quiet one; I slept well having taken a half of one of those sleeping pills that you used to swear by and certainly helped you. I remember but a few weeks ago when I would be having one of my restless nights, you knew I was awake and leaning over would pass me a pill and the bottle of water "Take this" you would whisper. I did as I was told and sleep would arrive and thankfully not leave for a while. I miss so much about you but the nights are still the hardest, I miss the stillness of your breathing next to me. Very lonely in the small hours now.

Yes, a quiet one. I began the day with the cuppa and this week's episode of Desperate Housewives.

A little routine I've developed for myself now. A little later, I gave the house a good late, spring clean. Good to slowly get things in a semblance of order, I dusted and vacuumed, sorted out the piles of laundry and wait for it, even got the cloths and disinfectant sprays earning their keep in the bathroom. Yep you can pick your spiritual self up off the celestial floor now, Russ cleaning the bathroom I will say it again, Russ, that's me, cleaning the bathroom! Another earthbound miracle has occurred! I expect miracles are one a penny your way but here we shall have to stick with a polish of the basin taps... for now. A trip to Sainsbury's for the weekly shop followed early afternoon then home to some reading and a doze.

As time goes on life does quite a good job at readjusting itself as I plus Oscar, Leo, Andy, your Mum and all your friends and family begin to live without you. Speaking just for me I do feel a lot calmer, no not a lot calmer, more at peace with us. By that I am not about to reject life and go into a Buddha like trance state throwing away all physical cares as I exchange the shorts and baggy shirt for long flowing yellow robes, sandals and happily singing "My Sweet Lord" at every available opportunity whilst banging tunelessly on my newly acquired tambourine. What I am saying is life is setting new parameters as different routines and structures emerge. I would still do anything for you to be here ; I really would but the you who was happy, boisterous, and enthusiastic with the sexiness, vitality and passion that I fell in love with. That's the you, not the shell of a woman that the illness reduced you too.

Ah well, impossible requests aside the sun is out, bike ride now then time for tea. A little earlier to bed tonight as Harry Potter takes over tomorrow. Remember the studio tour you booked last October when we were in Exeter? Silly girl, you must be cursing yourself now! Actually are you allowed to do that in your neck of the woods? Joking aside will let you know how it goes. Avril is taking your place so all in all it will be an eventful day! Love you. Xx

08:29pm 21st April

A quiet Saturday night unfolds. I've just cooked some mince along with a bowl of noodles with garlic and tomatoes. I have enough for two so if you're free do pop in? I have an extra wine glass handy too. Do try, feeling a little lonely sitting here. All very silly isn't it? We can't change anything but... I really miss you still and always. XX Nite.

12:55pm 23rd April

Jenny, you missed a good one! The Harry Potter tour just south of Watford at Leavesden studios!! We went we toured we enjoyed! We set off at 1.pm, the morning had been bad for me, the feelings again which had surfaced on Saturday night. I went for a long bike ride to exercise away the tears of regret, the ever present feelings of you not being here and how I should have done more not just at the end but over the time that we were together? Oh the ifs and buts crawl out of the subconscious to attack at the most inappropriate of times!

Any way I pulled myself out of the negativity of over thinking, collected an excited Leo before driving to Oscar's There he was all ready waiting outside with your Mum all smiles. He was walking towards the car before we'd stopped. Ready to go? I think so! Wow was he excited! Your Mum and Andy waved us off and we drove across the village to collect Avril your old friend who I only have met twice briefly before. There she stood small compact and full of energy. The tell it like it is Avril jumped into the car armed with mobile and a packet of cigarettes in hand. Off we drove stopping at the local shop to buy some provisions. The boys came out with sliced turkey, snickers bars and a box of After Eights which we managed to stop them eating the whole of on the journey up. Avril being a teacher has a natural affinity with kids and knew exactly how to talk to the boys and soon had them in hysterics with her attitudes to stuff, life whatever you want to call it. Relaxed sure but she established herself quickly and got them on her wavelength but with the respect due too.

We got to the Studios with no problems, and as we pulled into the car park there were gasps from the boys as from the distance rising above a wall we could see the top of the night bus situated close to what looked like the Privet Drive houses. Fantasy hits reality and worlds intertwine as we eased into our car parking space.

With an hour to go before our allotted tour we ended up in the Harry Potter gift shop, oh if ever there was an excuse to open the wallet or unzip the purse this was it, we all disappeared in a flurry of unpaid credit card bills eyes popping out cartoon like transfixed by the Potter power of merchandise to satisfy the cravings from Hufflepuff to Gryffindor desires satisfied. Avril bought a pile of souvenirs, for her son she said despite him only being six months old!

Soon we were in the queue and through the doors where we were given a brief overview of the Harry Potter Franchise and shown some of the posters that advertise the films all over the world. Another set of doors opened and the sense of anticipation amongst the kids not to mention us adults was electric as we were ushered into a cinema and shown a short information film hosted by Daniel, Rupert and Emma all about the tour, then yes the cinema screen is raised and we see before us the huge wooden double doors that within seconds swing open to reveal the Hogwarts banqueting hall in all its magical glory. Sighs and exhales of awed breath from the roomful of us excited visitors.

Are you enjoying this Jenny? Perhaps reading over my shoulder as I type out Harry Potter memories just for you? Do you regret not being here being with us yesterday or with me today? All four of us were so conscious of you and what you would have been like in JK Rowling land. So silly so sad so selfish... any way back to Hogwarts.

The great Hall beckoned us in, full of props and costumes from the films, and the actual set where all the scenes were filmed over the ten year period. We all took plenty of photos before being ushered through to the rest of the exhibition. To a devoted Harry Potter fan which Oscar professed himself to be several times on the walk round there was nothing that could not be seen, touched or photographed. From models, set recreations to an endless list of Potter paraphernalia, nothing was missed out. Highlights so far? Well the aforementioned night bus culminating in the visits to Privet Drive was amazing and the only part of the exhibition to be located outside where we also took a breather for some rather expensive glasses of butter beer! Tasted like cream soda to me but hey I spoil the fantasy!!

As the twilight of the exhibition approached we entered the charmed magical world of Diagon Alley! Lit by the softest of lighting we all strolled up the walkway taking in the beautifully recreated shops, from potions to wands and books by Gilderoy Lockhart crying out to be noticed we tried to take this magical world in. Our over exerted digital cameras and phones did their best. We saw the exit doors rising before us but not before the actual model of Hogwarts took centre stage glistening in a room of its own. Life-size no. Impressive? Yes!

We spent a good hour in the gift shop that by pure coincidence is the first room one enters after the exhibition exit, yep as if by magic, plenty of shopkeepers appeared to tempt and entice us to buy. We did! Avril bought Oscar and Leo wands they also posed for photos in wizard's costumes, I bought them a photo each. The Winchester Wizards!

Home time and talk of Harry Potter as we negotiated a rain swept visibility impaired M25. A stop at Fleet Services for a McDonald's tea, before home was on the horizon. We arrived as dusk set in. Avril home, Oscar home to his excited "Tell us all!" Gran and us two home. As Leo settled down he unsurprisingly watched a little Harry Potter and the Chamber of Secrets, new Ron Weasley wand in hand.

It was a fantastic day; there was chat, laughter and above all, joy. You silly lady. I have never seen your son so happy and enthused. Ah that pang of regret again and I think now of wanting to take you by the hand and look at you, just feel you near and hold you close, never let you go. Don't like it now you not here. With that sweetie pie, I go now. Speak later. XX

07:40pm 23rd April

It has two calendar months since you left. Eight weeks without you and perhaps I ought to admit to myself now, finally now, that you are actually dead. Yes dead, is there any other way to approach this now? You are not coming back. Using words or phrases that imply that you left gives me the hope that you are soon going to come bustling through the door, and I will see you again. No, you are dead and to quote John Cleese, "You have ceased to be, is no more, bereft of life it rests in peace" See my point? However, I would never refer to you as an "IT" or that you are a

Parrot! You died and expelled and rejected life and that was your choice. To me a wrong choice asI would have looked after you in my Groundhog Day world and would have got it right eventually so we could take that yellow brick road to our little Castle in the Sky! I can dream the dream? Speak tomorrow. Off to Kent for work.

08:39am 24th April

And yes, I am in Kent in a lovely pub styled country hotel, The Dog and Bear in Lenham just outside Maidstone. You know you are in for a relaxing time when you have to think for yourself i.e. the room you are in can only be accessed by the good old fashioned key, yep the metal type! I am sitting in the bar enjoying a pint of cider, eager couples walk past looking longingly at menus after being told of the forty five minute wait for a table. To the left is the public bar where there is a football match on the big screen. A quiet bunch of supporters of teams watch attentively waiting for a goal. Elsewhere the acolytes of Rupert Murdoch are counting their cash as they reap in the subscription public view packages. Goal! Ching ching!! To my right a new resident of the village is making his presence felt both as a businessmen and a local resident. His wife sits opposite him and listens to the mutterings of the self-deluded. "I spoke with him, I'm on it, I'm on everything!" and more words of wisdom. "Don't worry; all we need to do is marinade the chicken and turkey together, perfect for the housewarming!" Clearly an invite to the whole village?

Hey ho, I have no right to judge others. However when you are sitting in the bar on your own… I went for a yomp earlier in the little hamlet of Boughton Malherbe. This blink and you miss it curio was the epitome of stillness. I pulled up next to a ream of sunflower fields that stretched towards the heavens (can you see them?!!) got out my walking pole and strolled off into the wilderness of an early evening Spring day. It is lambing season and I passed fields of yews sheltering their newly born. Mothers very protective of their young and as I approach they run towards the fence separating the fields from the country lane. The stare, the look as mother yews with bulging sacks of baby milk dragging along the grass gave me the look. "Keep away!" was the feeling stretching across the wool kitted mothers of the Kent countryside. Lambs not bothered they skipped around jumping in the air performing circular motions of joyous fun. Happy happy times and in the mind's eye of the young, not a sniff of the inevitable mint sauce.

I strolled back to the car inhaling the freshness of the evening the smell of the honeysuckle drifting across fields of the Garden of England. Step by step I had thoughts of you and me walking through this idyllic bliss hand in hand you fresh faced and illness free enjoying the quiet and we properly planning a future. I would grip you tightly to me and we would breathe in the beauty of the countryside and walk on together. Always together. Understand? Can I dream just for a little while? Nite. Xx

07:59am 26th April

Morning, apologies for not being in touch yesterday, my work at the Hilton in Maidstone did keep me quite busy. The day started in rain swept Lenham; I made my way to the solitary dining room of the aforementioned Dog and Bear. I sat there with my glass of orange juice waiting to place my breakfast order, soon a feisty Scottish lady appeared from the swinging kitchen door, armed with pen and pad "Good morning sir, tea or coffee?" "Oh tea please" I replied. "Very well, and for your breakfast?" I asked for a couple of poached eggs and a round of wholemeal toast. This seemed to go down well and within minutes I was presented with a solitary piece of toast, a quite cold piece of solo toast taking centre stage on the plate next to my newly delivered pot of tea. As I looked at the piece of toast a hand appeared within my eye line brandishing another

168

plate with a single poached egg clearly marked for companionship with the other solo item that had just been delivered. "Excuse me" I said tentatively, "I did ask for a round of toast, would it be possible to have another couple of slices, also maybe another poached egg?" there was a pause, "really?" she said giving me that look that reminds you of being a child at a friends house as you eye a particularly delicious looking piece of chocolate cake and getting into trouble Oliver style, "You want more? Why? Do you have hollow legs or something?" a shocked mother would say. "Well, if possible" I utter back in the dining room of the Dog and Bear only too conscious of the world food shortages that dominate the newspaper headlines when there are no reality shows on TV. "Very well, I will see what I can do!" and off she scuttles through the perpetually swinging kitchen doors. I sit reading my book half listening for the pop of a toaster and the crack of an eggshell or two but, nothing. My imagination works overtime as I picture Mrs Feisty Scottish lady charging around a field desperately trying to catch up with her solo chicken pleading for her feathered friend to drop one. Which came first the chicken or the egg? Ho ho, but I did get a big basket of toast delivered to my table along with not one but two poached eggs presented with a smile and a complimentary bottle of tomato sauce! The eggs were yummy and I tucked in before embarking on the toast. As I picked up the first piece the kitchen door swung open again and out blustered Mrs Feisty clearly accompanied by her other half Mr. Feisty. As I buttered that first tempting slice I watched the couple clearing the recently breakfasted table to the opposite of mine. "Look at this!" utters Mrs. Feisty; "the toast is untouched, not more complaints about the bread surely?" "No more than usual" mumbles Mr. Feisty in between wipes of the table. I look at my freshly buttered piece of wholemeal; think for a second then bite in. I crunch the first mouthful in tune with the rhythmic motions of the Feisty cloths. I continue to eat, butter spread, toast eaten. With a contented sigh I stand and make my leave from the dining room sidestepping the tidying couple. Tables cleaned but the full basket of complained about toast remains fixed on the table opposite mine, I take a glance. White bread! That explains it! Off I go to Maidstone and a day of so called work.

All these little adventures eh? Feeling jealous up there in your resting place? Wish you were with me on one of our little trips? It is getting easier but I do miss you on the overnight stays, we used to have such fun and when we were away from the confines of the village that in many ways held you in a grip of regret, guilt and confusion that day to day life seemed inflict, you were Jenny, the human being, the sexy fun loving woman that loved life. That is what I want and need to remember, it makes me smile. Have a good day, speak soon. XX

11:07 am 28th April

Hmm, the rain pours down outside, maybe it is true what they say about the April showers! Good news I have started going back to the gym. I went for the first time this week since you died. Maybe I had just got out of the habit but I was slightly apprehensive as my most recent memories are of our visits. There I would be on the bicycle pedalling away, I would glance in the mirror and you would be on the cross trainer a few rows back, iPod on, concentrating fiercely, hair tied back, dressed in your black work out gear. So, I was worried about that which is silly as I have been going to the Leisure Centre for the past ten or so years and the majority of times without you! Beginning to get back into some sort of routine has to be done, I'm doing my best. Actually I thoroughly enjoyed my visit and spent a long time languishing in the sauna, a sweat and a doze. What could be better? Well....

Yesterday morning I woke just before 7.am, got up made a cuppa woke Leo, then it hit me. I hadn't thought about you!! By that the last sixty odd days had been brought to life with the "she's not here

171

any more" that sentence screaming its way through the birdsong, like a dodgy car engine failing to start. I would get up; my hand would brush your redundant dressing gown as I reach for mine. In the bathroom I am surrounded by your stuff, in the kitchen I would fill your kettle always remembering to filter the water like you taught me. Today all this as before but I wasn't thinking of you. I thought of the day ahead, thought of preparing Leo's breakfast, plus the money for his lunch. Time easing the past?

Despite this I am aware that there is a grumbling anger within me. For instance on this apparently positive start to Friday morning, I didn't know how to reactivate my Microsoft outlook account on my iPad after I had reset it after a software glitch. No big deal really but something trivial triggers the frustration and anger like a faulty kettle that has reached boiling point but can't switch off. "Oh for God's sake...." And on and on I go "I haven't got time for this...!" Leo was just finishing his breakfast. "Dad just chill with you?!" said with very little emotion as if he has accepted the way I can now behave. He goes to school and I wish him a distracted goodbye. Then I feel bad about that, neglecting my son, who should be seeing a buoyant and happy Dad wishing him a wonderful day at school, not be on the tense receiving end of a man seemingly on the verge of a nervous breakdown over an email account., which obviously got fixed in a matter of minutes one I'd taken a step back.

I know that you are dead Jenny and know that you were so ill so dreadfully ill and the inevitability of the cure will have repercussions for the rest of us always but I worry for these flashes of anger and impatience which just hit. Something so trivial can trigger an outburst, someone standing in a shop doorway blocking the path, being behind a driver doing thirty in a forty mile zone, being in a queue at the train station and the person in front renewing a railcard for themselves plus buying a super saver non refundable away day return ticket for a proposed journey in 2014. Light the blue touch paper Jenny and I'm fizzing away internally. The people to suffer are those close to me. Leo has said to his Mum quite rightly that "Dad always seems angry." Last night when I got back from a rain swept but bracing dog walk he was full of smiles and gave me a big hug as I was leaving. I'm still taking that deep breath. Anger Management. Anger at what? There is a potpourri of emotions. I can defend my behaviour in a way, your death, the person I thought I had decades with stretching far far down our yellow brick road will take a while to accept emotionally despite the reality checks but I need to filter my behaviour and give the support to Leo which I'm not doing. A reason, not an excuse. False smiles are fine, he can see through that. He sensed the tension in our house when you were still alive, you would put on a brave face to hide your darkness but he knew. I now have to address the same issue and stop myself sliding into a self piteous world of bitterness and sadness. Believe me its there waiting quietly for me to unlock the door! Recrimination has the patience of a saint (Just ask if you happen to pass one!) it always knows it will get a say eventually. So, keep an eye on me and give me a little kick if you spot the signs that you know so well. As always Jenny, I love you, despite everything. Okay on with the day. Deep breath. Xx

03:20pm 28th April

Okay, I write the above, I try to, try to what? I'm just back from a bike ride which normally does me good when I feel like this. How can I have a few days of accepting your death and the realisation that life must go on and concentrate on being a good father which as we discussed very much on the back burner as is everything? I walked into the house a few minutes ago and felt as if I had stepped way out of the reality that I am trying to put into place. Standing in the lounge the tears began to flow as I am confronted with our past and my present, it's crippling, the pain and the anger have attacked again and I don't know what to do about it. I don't want to be reminded of anything yet I don't want to forget. Things are closing in Jenny and what step in the grieving process I am at, I have no idea, no idea at all. Whatever I do whatever steps I put into place to deal with this and deal with you not being here are quashed by a fresh demon of the subconscious finding its feet feeding me the dangerous pictures, the images of you locking the backdoor walking upstairs and holding the knife, running the bath. They laugh as I dwell on your sadness that you have to resort to this and my guilt and sense of failure is so strong despite the reality that you would have found a way to end your pain whatever we had done. Christ beautiful lady I am in a bad place, a bad place. I feel I am losing my grip. It shouldn't be like this, I wrap my arms around myself to quell the despair despite knowing that if you were still alive and unwell things would be far from happy. Strained relations between you and me, Leo and Oscar, Ellie and me worrying about the effect on our son, pressures would mount at work. Our life would be purgatory, I know that, we all know that but that doesn't stop what I am feeling. I've locked the rose tinted specs away but curiously they are always on the bureau waiting to be put on, their job to guide me on the short sited path to a contentment that didn't exist on the morning of

23rd February. I am beginning to think that I am going insane… xx

08:52pm 30th April

Hello, hi, what you up to? I am in the rather cramped bar of the Hilton Hotel on the outskirts of Stansted airport. Yet another couple of days away this time the away is Essex. I am sitting next to a man with one of those car engine laughs, a born entertainer he tells story after story to his two companions, each anecdote broken with the turn of the key. Nope still not starting, perhaps he should check his dipstick. The pint is going down well. "Yet another pint Russell?" I hear you tut tutting. God I wish I could hear you and see you. Yep I know I am the classic example of the broken record so sorry. The weekend was not the best but I'm going to put a lot of it down to the weather, it rained and rained and yes pissed down with a few harsh winds thrown in for good measure. That sums up the outside world and pretty much what was going on internally for yours truly for a lot of the time. I can beat this, I can get through this but from day to day I never know what is going to strike. It begins quietly, laundry, tidying, recycling, and shopping all the things that need doing after a busy week. Done, I return to the empty house and like the aforementioned stuck record. "What is the point?" No can't help it. It returns like a frustrated boomerang that I can't catch and break. I go cycling and the grief takes over and the tears flow battling the raindrops for pride of place.

Then the sun comes out I am cooking a roast for Leo and Oscar late on Sunday afternoon. I listen to their laughter and things get better. Food eaten Wii games played Harry Potter wands produced as one of the movies crops up on the TV. We thrill to the escapades and the Dementors strike as roast potatoes are devoured and Yorkshire puddings get filled with gravy.

I drive Oscar home, he is quiet as usual and I want to ask him how he is doing but I don't. Instead we exchange small talk about school and DVDs. When I drop him off at your Mum's he turns waves and smiles before slowly walking in. Your Mum sends a text through saying he had a fun evening.

I wake at 2.am. I can't get back to sleep. Seconds then minutes tick by and eventually as the hours take over I fall back into a fitful sleep and dream.

I'm on a conference call, it's Sunday afternoon and I need to call the Wi-Fi installer bosses about an issue at Hilton Newbury North. For some reason I am chairing this call and driving along a terraced road on the coast. At a changing set of traffic lights I stop and as the hands free discussions continue I hear a "hello" I turn, you sit next to me dressed in a black trouser suit with white blouse peeking through. "Russ, you need to sleep, come here" and I take my hands off the wheel as you curl up in my arms. I grip you so tightly it hurts but the sensation is so real. The conference voices drone on and I hug you tighter. I pull away and look into your eyes, they are clear and the light shines through. In the reflection of the brightness I see my bed then I'm in my bed as the early morning birdsong takes over. "No, no, please this should be the dream!" and I reach out my hand and for a few seconds the car gently purrs and you are smiling. "I really am so sorry" your voice resonates, "sleep, Russ please" and I do holding your hand. Peace. I look at the clock my hand clenched with nothing. 7am. Here we go again. Bugger. Xx

09:57am 1st May

Jenny, I've just been attacked by a shower, the demon shower! For the casual observer it looked like your normal type of shower head silvery in appearance, very much attached to its Fawcett. So as you do I adjusted the height made sure the nozzle was aimed not in my general direction and on went the water. Then as if auditioning for a role in Anaconda 2 the shower head led by the silvery dildo like hose leapt off the wall hook dived

178

into the bath and began a series of exaggerated circular movements spraying very cold water over me and then onto the floor. I scrabbled against the jet like sprays and fiddled with the taps and eventually switched them off which for some reason is never easy in a hotel. Which way to turn, left or right? Hmm that's another question to be addressed later. Okay, I eventually had my shower and mopped up the floor, but the whole incident reminded me of our October 2011 stay in The White Hart in Exeter. Sitting on the bed we were, you in full Harry Potter mode trying to make the studio tour booking forgetting that you had started running the bath. It only seemed like a few minutes since the taps had been switched on however I think the excitement of getting to grips with Sorting Hats and imaginary Quidditch tournaments had taken your mind off the approaching radox moments. So not to feel left out, the contents of the bath came to us water seeped across the bathroom floor and under the door and then you noticed it. " Christ the bath!" you yelled, leaping up flinging open the door and diving for a bunch of towels, throwing them on to the couple of inches of water as you waded over to turn off the taps. I phoned Housekeeping who were marvellous, two sprightly ladies arrived instantaneously like agents from the Men in Black movies, no panic, no fuss as if they were used to a potential flood on a daily basis. In between supplies of fresh towels, free flowing buckets and mops and reassurances to you that the floor wasn't about to give in denying us the potential for a rather spectacular entrance to the lounge bar, everything was slowly tided back to normal. I can't remember whether you had a bath but later we had a rather rushed check out. For the best we thought.

And The White Hart is still standing, will have to visit again on my next trip to the West Country. I'll let you know when I am going, in case you happen to be passing overhead. Work now, speak later. Xx

07:52pm 1st May

Oh, here we are, back in the bar of the Stansted Hilton. As I ordered my second pint I had the sudden urge to have a quick chat with you. The thing is I find myself talking to you a lot especially during the times when I am away and enjoying the anonymity of hotel life. So I put the pint down went back to my room and collected my HP notebook. Back to my little table strategically positioned in the corner by the rear window (visions of Jimmy Stewart in a wheelchair with a telescope getting excited at the supposed criminal goings on of his neighbours is an image that springs to mind. If I start referring to my friend Harvey, do let me know!). So, what is new? Not a lot. I've been busy doing nothing which is really no fault of mine. I was told to come up to Essexville, very important work you understand to get these Hiltons programmed into the Wi-Fi generation of the 21st century, get them to understand the free to user service that is being introduced nationwide. "Free to user?" I hear you cry? Indeed when sites and hotel chains eventually go this way this does significantly decrease the need for people like me to visit and with my current contract now being renewed on just a six monthly basis… some food leading to too much thought.

Enough of that as I come to the end of my busy doing nothing. It is like being on holiday in a way. For instance to begin at the beginning, I had a lie in followed by a scrambled egg breakfast and my frightening encounter with the angry shower. A leisurely drive to the outskirts of Braintree and a visit to the Hilton where all I had to do was see if the landing pages would accept the free to user internet access codes. They did, have the manager to sign the paperwork and I was away. That was it so a short drive to Braintree followed by a stroll around the small and compact town. Just a brief walk around Jenny before the welcoming Hilton beckoned fifteen minutes along the dual carriageway. To Living Well for a workout, a doze and here I am, talking to you, fresh faced and content with my tiredness knowing I will sleep well tonight, comfortable in the stress free ambiance of a homogenised hotel.

Would I class myself as a bar fly? In the past, perhaps. I do know the bar etiquette though. Now my trips to pubs and bars are infrequent but I do enjoy the atmosphere of the hustle and bustle, the jostling for attention from the regular guests who think they should be served first. For example, a few feet away from me are two chaps from Birmingham who have just been approached by bar supervisor Sonya. "It is good to see you again pet, I am all the better when you smile!" Sonya does smile passes them two pints of Stella and proffers the bar menu. They ignore the offer now intently texting to possible loved ones north of the M42. Next to them a couple staring into space sipping their drinks, no talk just the resigned acceptance of another day passed? Do you think we would have got like that Jenny? The past was well trodden but our future was undecided.

Enough, time away, like a holiday, feel tired but comfortably tired. Time to just not think and give the subconscious a rest which does get the creative juices flowing. That's given me a happy thought! Now now, no mock shock "Mr Cook!" looks. Happy times, happy places. Nite sexy! XX

08:41pm 3rd May

Evening sexy from a rain drenched Kings Worthy! I've just wasted two hours of my life. "How?" I hear you ask. I sat through the film "Captain America. The First Avenger" without falling asleep or just giving up on life (sorry a cheap joke I know). You and I loved a good film; we went to the cinema more times than I can remember and watched so many DVDs and premieres on Sky Movies. In the early days of our relationship we had gone to a Saturday night showing of Avatar in Basingstoke. One of those rare evenings with time just for us. Oscar was at a sleepover with friends and off we went. Did we go out to dinner? Sort of if you count a couple of whoppers at Burger King a fulfilling meal for a newly in love couple discovering themselves on the verge of a 3D experience! Back to your flat after and a late Saturday night turned into a lazy Sunday morning. For our post coital breakfast I produced croissants filled with bacon and cheese. We munched on those, sipped our tea and watched at your request "You Don't Mess with the Zohan" Oh, so very good! A film I had dismissed previously had me howling with laugher as I held your hand, not believing my good fortune at having found you as the talents of Adam Sandler as a super hero unfolded on the flat screen in front of us. Much better than Captain America!

So, watching a bad film tonight so formulaic in its approach to storytelling reminds me of those happy times with you. That is not a bad thing. Time for a goodnight but before I go I remember the excitable evening when you produced a copy of the newly released DVD of "The Time Travellers Wife". A film we were both keen to see. We saw, we watched…. we were disappointed at the dullness of a badly told tale. Not a patch on the book. Late evening as we got ready for bed "Hmm, not bad eh?" say I, thinking of the price in full that you had paid for the DVD. "Indeed" you said. "Shall I use the bathroom first?" you uttered. I didn't argue. I was just happy to be with you, fresh into our relationship and happy that you had conquered your illness and were enjoying life. Holding hands physically and mentally. No barriers in those early days. Lights out but for you then in the early months of 2010 the on switch was easy to press... Nite beautiful lady.

08:35 am 4th May

Morning, I woke far too early though not through panic or missing you (no offence!) maybe I'd just had enough sleep? Lay in bed for a bit and stared at the ceiling, put on the news. Another week is near an end. What have you been up to recently, you have been very quiet! Actually I'm feeling a little quiet today, almost as If I have nothing to say. Think it shows! Bit like real life really. Everyone has a day like that or a day like this. My turn. Time to think about work. Off to Southampton in a bit. I like Fridays! Speak later. Xx

02:14pm 4th May.

I was just thinking in a rather proud sort of way about how much I love you. It makes me smile and in a good way. I am so pleased we found each other, despite the outcome. You with your extraordinary femininity and natural beauty chose me. Thank you. I know that we made each other happy and I treasure our memories. Okay, time to wipe away a little tear, that's allowed. Xx

03:50pm 6th May

Hi, all good? Just over halfway through the Bank Holiday, a few days into May and we are yet to see a glimpse of sun. Thankfully it hasn't rained today; I've just got back from an invigorating dog walk, ground reasonably dry unlike Friday afternoon when I returned home wearing mud boots! Leo and Oscar are in Winchester, I gave them a lift in at 1.pm, and they have gone in to meet friends, all very secretive between the two of them. We arrived at your Mum's house at 12.55 I was pleased with myself for being early for a change but Oscar was agitated, "Can we go soon please we are supposed to be there by one!" I caught the last few words as he was walking out of the door leaving me in mid sentence with your Mum; we looked at each other and smiled. Leo and Oscar meeting two girls, one, Julia, I think Oscar is going out with, you should be proud as a Mum, your son is blossoming. We parked by the Bus station and both boys turned to me "You are going now aren't you?" as they turned and walked towards Shakeaway "Off to get the papers?" "Yes" I replied turning to go towards the high street. The boys didn't give me a backward look and quite right too. I understand Julia is bringing her friend Emma, well so Leo told me rather shyly earlier. I will update you later, but don't embarrass your son Jenny!!

I took all your jewellery over to your Mum's. She asked for it, I think amongst the costume jewellery there are certain bits that are of value, family bracelets and necklaces. She wants to find the pieces, sell them and put the money in a trust fund for Oscar. Collected both boxes from the right hand side of the dressing table, a little more of your earthly personality leaves chez Cook. Is this a good thing Jenny? Do you know I think it probably is, I mentioned to you last week of the clash of past and present, a past dead and buried if you will pardon the bad joke and a present that at the moment I can't take a full role in until I begin to shrug off the old skin. At times it's a very comfortable skin, so easy to wallow in chrysalis like dreams and impossible hopes, surround myself with you. However that results in a one way journey as we have discussed before. For me to be able to spread my wings butterfly like, your memory and presence need to be reduced to a manageable quantity. Therefore, how to start? Tell you what I will go for a bike ride and have a think…. Won't keep you in suspense for long. Hope your Sabbath is going well. Xx

08:55pm 6th May

Hello, I am still thinking, so keep the suspense alive (sorry!) Give me a little while longer? There is a lot I want to say to you but it is getting late and I'm tired. So want to talk to you now, just to get your take on things but I wouldn't do either you or me justice. Can we talk tomorrow? Goodnight X

09:39am 8th May

Morning. How are you? I know that we need to chat about your stuff but time for work in a minute, so will attempt to address the issues tonight. Sorry to keep you waiting. Just to let you know, I am struggling today, missing you big time. I always told you I didn't like big rollercoaster rides, currently whizzing downhill; I've got my seatbelt on, preparing for a bumpy day. Love you.

Afternoon. It is still raining here, thankfully me a little better today, though very tired. I had another dream about you the night before last. This time you and I were at a health spa, both of us in robes standing outside his and hers saunas. I about to go into my sauna stand in front of you and ask "are you sure you are not going anywhere?" "I've told you, I'm staying!" you say with a reassuring smile. "Are you sure?! You will be here when I get back?" I continue as if unable to stop. "Yes!" this time you are laughing. "Don't be a twit, now go and enjoy, see you in a minute!!" I wake up, enough said.

Now back to the unanswered questions. To declutter or stay cluttered? Stay in the present of our past? As I write you coats hang nearby still on the connecting door to the porch. Upstairs I walk into our/my bedroom (delete as applicable). Opening the bedside chest of draws and all your socks, underwear and bras stare back at me, all washed, and immaculately folded and of no use to me whatsoever. As a point of interest, some of my underpants have several holes in rather exposed places but I see no reason that a situation will come to pass when I am going to be so desperate for underclothing that I find my hands reaching tentatively towards a pair of your panties (before you say anything I am not going to go there! Any way you were wearing them at the time!) as I dress for that important business meeting. So it makes sense to bag them all up and take to the nearest charity bin? Yes? Okay then. My attention turns towards the wardrobe; one side is full of your beautifully ironed shirts, blouses and assorted tops. The other, jeans, trousers, dresses, suits, all immaculately ironed and hung up as if suspended in time awaiting instructions that are never forthcoming from the recently departed owner. I push through the trousers and am confronted with the back of the wardrobe. I tap the hardboard hoping for an imaginary door guiding me toward a lamp post silhouetting a snow filled land, perhaps where you have escaped to, hunting the Turkish delight, chasing the Lion and avoiding the witch? Sadly nothing, however hard I tap, just the hollowness of the wood reverberating back to reality and the abandoned clothes. Enough of this! Yes, it is time Jenny; I do need to move on. How does a drive at the weekend to the British Heart Foundation sound?

03:25pm 9th May

Okay. Stage one. Coats removed from behind the door. Baby steps? Dog walk now. Speak later. Xx

10:03am 10th May

Hi, just to let you know I have bagged up all your shoes and boots and they will be on their way to charity very shortly. I have also included the big pair of fluffy booty slippers that I bought you for Christmas, no point me hanging onto them is there? Nothing else to say at the moment. I am sure you can imagine how I feel. Xx

02:45 pm 11th May

Afternoon! What a day. Guess what, the sun is out!! This is the major revelation, nothing else. Makes things a lot easier doesn't it, warmth and sunnier climes. Just to let you know, I did go through with it yesterday, loaded the three bags of shoes into the car, battled the rain showers and went down to that car park on the edge of Andover Road where they always hold the boot sales of a Sunday. The big red metal tub similar in shape but not size to an American mailbox emblazoned with the white lettered British Heart Foundation logo stands in the corner of the car park. The door resembling a large eager robotic mouth eagerly accepted the bags as I proffered them forward, drop, clang, mouth shut. Thank you very much! As the last of the bags disappeared from view I waited for the rain and chill winds to disappear to be replaced by the golden sunlight and sweet sound of early summer birdsong; as a thank you for my charitable deeds! Nope it continued to piss down and if anything the cold winds seemed to pick up a bit. You could have had a word?! All for the good eh? Little bits of you going to help others? I think so.

04:59pm 13th May

Another weekend passes in the blink of hay fever filled eyes. To have at last, a weekend without stormy weather, both internally and externally made the topping up of the antihistamines a pleasure! Saturday was spent in the house and I continued to rearrange the space around me, cupboards cleared out, clothes bagged up, out with the old but not in with the new. I found the whole thing surprisingly therapeutic, that is creating space giving the house room to breathe which it needs not just by opening the windows and letting the outside world in (come to think about it , that's not a bad idea!) but creating space in my mind to move forward, I am sure you will agree, a cleansing process.

I thought about it as I tackled the garden in the afternoon. With a sense of vigour I got the spade out and attacked the weeds that were dominating the pathway and flower beds. Dig, dig, dig, green bag filled, each wipe of the sweaty brow resulting in another space cleared. A good couple of hours later I saw a little semblance of order and thoughts began to grow of what I can plant to bring some colour to my little patch of green. So Jenny, change inside and outside....

So with changes going on each day with the intention of pushing forward to a calmer place the time has come for me too to take a step away from this, my letter to you Jenny. To say that my almost daily conversations with you have helped me come to terms with your death would be the understatement of the...understatement of what a year? A lifetime of a lifelong eternity?!! However my witterings are becoming commonplace and repetitive. My day in a way can solely focus on what I want to say to you which cotton wools me from reality, the reality that you are not here any more and never will be. Life is put on hold as I sit down to type and the words pour out weaving their magical pattern forming a life on the page that I wish was still here. I will never get over the fact that you and I could have done so much, ignited our dreams into a bonfire of the vanities that would have surpassed both of our expectations. You would be free of the illness and we would have marched together as equals. Two mates, united souls always smiling and encountering life together. That is what we had promised each other. Your illness made you break that promise and I am coming to terms with that, slowly.

I need to spread my wings and fly (actually I know this is not practically possible due to something called gravity, could you have a word, ask those wing owning guardian chaps how its done? Perhaps a little extra celestial project for you when you're not taking Fritz out on one of those eternal walks?) and to use that oft quoted phrase yet again, move on, take a stride forward, take a deep breath and put away the thoughts the ever recurring thoughts of the what if...

This is not a goodbye, not even a farewell, it's a gentle acknowledgement of a time that is now past and a see you soon. I will pop back now and again to update you, especially where Oscar is concerned but,I need to concentrate on the living, the moment of the present. I look over my shoulder for one final time to see you walk towards me and give me a gentle goodbye kiss, our lips brushing before you step back and give me that dazzling smile as you wave farewell. I turn towards the paths of the unknown. Which way? Little steps leading into confident strides but Jenny, remember whatever happens in the future a part of me will always acknowledge "you were always the woman to and for me". Au revoir beautiful lady.

07:24 pm 13th May

It's all gone very quiet, just the gentle ticking of the clock…..

18:59pm 13th June.

Hello, you still about? Not flown off somewhere? It has been a month since I stepped back from our conversation to take a look at the bigger picture, and yes get some breathing space. I write tonight as I've just got back from the West Country with visits to Sidmouth and Exeter and the surrounding areas. I knew the two days would be a little bit of a challenge 'cos I don't need to wear the rose tinted spectacles when I think back to the times we spent walking, talking and just being…in the moment or more importantly in the West Country so to speak. In the never ending moment of being away from the stresses and strains of real life just for a few days. Funny but I didn't find Exeter that hard not even when walking past The White Hart hotel where we did the ghost hunt, nearly a year ago now, with you dragging me out of bed at midnight after you had befriended the night porter and persuaded him to give you and me the tour. Happy times seeing you in your element hanging on to every ghostly word said on our spooky tour. Clear eyed you and with a child's innocent curiosity at the spooky tales told to the tick tock of the witching hour. Good old Exeter, happy times eh?

Jenny, I thought I was being sensible by moving away from one of our favourite places and spending the night in Sidmouth. Sure we had been there together but only on brief visits, trips to Costa Coffee spring to mind, you bustling around the shops looking for the latest bargains whether presents of chocolate for your Mum or a browse at the kitchenware in the haberdashery shop. Yep, I was safe in Sidmouth so happily checked in to the Victoria Hotel free from memories of times past. Didn't quite work out like that! You see, I hadn't expected to find Sidmouth when it is devoid of sun on a cloud covered drizzle infested summers evening to be so damned depressing! There I was walking along the promenade wrapped up in coat and hat really feeling the cold as the wind battled for supremacy over the slightly pissed off sky and grey coloured utterly miserable uninviting sea. "No good" I thought, so decided to go back to the hotel and enjoy the comforts of the warmth of the hotel bar and a glass of something bad for me. Result? Peace and contentment? Um, not quite. I turned 46 recently as I am sure you are aware, so technically I am probably halfway through my life if I am being extremely charitable to myself. Well on walking to the hotel bar in search of the always refreshing pint of cider I was confronted by a room full of people who made me feel that I should have been wearing nappies and in search of a night-time's supply of Farley's rusks and free pouring warm ready to drink full fat milk. I ordered a drink from a man in full evening dress who bowed reverentially as he reached for my chosen beverage. Actually I wasn't sure whether he was going to get up again as in mid bow he seemed to freeze as if in practice for an Olympic style dive but lets put that down to the cold weather as he regained his composure not to mention his full height proffering me my bottle of cider with a smile and the offer of a crystal clean glass. I made my way to a free table, sat down and poured my drink. It was 8.pm and I was in the middle of the pre dinner drinks hour of the eternal mid-eighties holidaymakers. Women in evening dress, men in jacket and ties all supping double whiskeys or large gin and tonics with ice and the occasional slice. There was I in tee shirt, jeans and black leather jacket, trying to fit in. For a busy hotel bar everything was all quiet on the conversation front, drinks sipped, dead time to kill before dinner. Occasionally a watch was looked at and the ticking hands would then create a flurry of activity as dinner reservations needed to be honoured. And a couple would shuffle out ready for the starters, the main course, perhaps dessert and a nightcap before bed leading to the same routine again tomorrow. As all this carried on the Bar Manager he of the full evening dress proffered his expertise around the tables offering trays of little snacks.

Eventually he arrived at my table with the offer of a bread stick or two, perhaps a canapé? I politely declined. "Are you sure?" he retorted with the charm of the excitable Lurch from "The Addams Family. " It's just that we are trying to get rid of them". Enough. I finished my drink and made my way to my room. My single room. Hmm

I drifted off to sleep to the sound of the sea washing up onto the stone filled beach, I must say Jenny the bed was a single and a very small one at that, if we had been sharing you would have had to lie on top of me, I am sure we could have adapted! Actually slept quite well, waking quite early. Looking out across the view of the town from my hotel room, I was presented with greyness, rain, more rain. A solitary person wrapped up against the elements struggled along the promenade fulfilling the early morning commitment of a dog walk no doubt to the delight of her excitable border collie. It really was a clash of colours out there beyond my little window, the almost blinding greenness of the local cricket pitch and Bowling Green contrasting badly with the reality of the drabness of a seaside resort devoid of its summer rights. Like a David Hockney painting gone very wrong.

Breakfast beckoned and I made my way to the lounge. Room 305!" I announced to the chap manning the desk. "Good morning sir, is it just you wanting a table?" Jenny, I wanted to say "No! There are two, me and someone else. We will be eating together, at the same table!" I didn't, I haven't got that delusional but quietly said "yes, just me" and was shown to a small table by the window. I went through the usual routine, ordered tea "brown toast please and a round of bacon with two poached eggs?" I walked over to the buffet area with the intent of getting some orange juice queuing up behind an elderly lady who had lost her glasses and couldn't differentiate between the bowls of cereal and the jugs of juice. An embarrassing scene was avoided by the intervention of a sprightly waiter running over with newly found specs. No glass of sugar puffs for her! Back at my table I munched on my newly delivered toast listening to the excitable strains of Ravel's Bolero being pumped out across the room. I carried on munching took a bite of a tomato sauce covered poached egg looking around me as I did so. I was the youngest in the room. Every person sitting to the left and right of me was over eighty. It is rather disconcerting to watch a group of people eating bowls of cereal almost in rhythm to the dying strains of Ravel's most famous composition. A daily routine, crunch crunch chew, and swallow; serviettes tucked in under chins creating the illusion of an overfilled washing line, still and ready for that last minute iron. A different time Jenny, I'd stepped back into a bygone age of the shirt and tie breakfast, the newly printed copies of The Times nestling next to the coffee pots, all leading onto the awaiting dining room for mid morning refreshments with fondant fancies on plates placed carefully on doilies.

I felt underdressed and a bit of a rebel, I mean I had two buttons open on my shirt! Yeah, a bit of a rebel looking out of the window again as the drizzle made its home away from the dark skies. I'm 46 and on my own in a part of England long forgotten and only to be found on the dusty old VHS Ealing Film collection. Then again I am making presumptions. I sat in that lounge feeling lost and frustrated and missing you very much. The silence of Sidmouth got quite deafening at times but for some it will be a comfort, lives enjoyed over the decades before I even existed, still here and, excuse the pun, very much alive. The dawning realisation that without you I've become very much a husk, existing and getting on with things but just going through the motions. Maybe I should have stayed in Exeter at our favourite hotel? Then again that is like a comfort blanket as I would have been back in the happy times and reality is then kept very much at bay. Sidmouth, its rain drenched bleakness and stillness made me realise that I am still very much alive, you are not but I am. "There is much to do" I thought as I drove out of the seaside town. As I did so I sensed a little sun behind the clouds, back to the hustle and bustle of roads with two lanes and smart phones with a signal. See you soon, love you still x

THE END?

LOVE LETTER

Before Jenny and I got together we had a number of false starts. I fell in love with her within minutes of us first meeting in April 2006. I was approaching 40 had been married and divorced so it would be fair to say that I'd had a couple of trips around the block. But (there is that word again!) this was different. As soon as we started talking on that spring April morning I knew she was the one. I am not saying this with the benefit of hindsight and as I write the rose tinted glasses are locked away in a secure safe far far away along the yellow brick road keeping the lightning bolts and claps of eye opening thunder company! It just felt right; in every sense.

After our first meeting we didn't speak for eighteen months then a chance meeting in a park led to a few get togethers, talks in her flat and on one winters evening I confessed a little of my feelings as we sipped wine and munched on pizza. Yes I was attracted to her and Jenny the plain Jenny of her own description looked genuinely shocked that any man could find her attractive. The low self esteem raised its ugly head leading to her putting up her guard, up went the barriers and I was cast out into the emotional cold. However, living in the same small village, we continued to meet and one day after we had walked back from school together chatting, laughing and just having fun, I felt the urge to tell her how I felt, for real! Still she was reticent to meet up away from the safety of the school run or a chat in the park. What to do? In a moment of romantic madness I sat down and wrote a love letter, a love letter from the heart. It was something I needed to do. I wrote my feelings out on parchment paper placed my written emotions in an envelope and one Friday afternoon, posted it through her door. Home I went to wait for a response.

Dearest Jenny,

I can recall when we first chatted like it was yesterday. We first met in 2006 and walked home from school on that sunny morning.

I was immediately hooked by you, just being with you made me smile all day thinking how I had met a delightful and beautiful lady.

So, as time went on, I looked forward to our chats on street corners or in the school playground, the 202 more I got to know you, the more I realised how amazing you really are as a woman and a mother and I started falling for you. When I am with you, you make me feel alive right to the ends of every nerve in my body and how can I ignore that feeling?

I tried to convey this to you one evening as we sat in your flat. It is a difficult thing to bring up in conversation and you were very sweet in deflecting my mumbled attempts at expressing my feelings.

What I am trying to say, is that I'm crazy about you. Put simply, you take my breath away and I want the chance to see if we can grow this into something rich and as precious as pure gold. Believe me, I have tried to suppress this and put it down to a passing fancy but these feelings grow inside me every day and they will never go away.

Jenny, when you meet someone that you know you want to spend the rest of your life with, and love and look after, you want it to start as soon as possible. Love is so rare in this world; why not take this chance with me? See where we end up? I won't let you down and just being in your presence will make me the happiest man in the universe.

Don't be scared, if you want to take leap of faith, I will be there to catch and just love you. If you don't want to leap, I understand, but tread softly, for you tread on my dreams.

There was no response, nothing, the days and months passed and it was then that I realised that I had done all I could. It was time to find a sense of closure.

COOK'S WORLD COLUMNS AND SOCIAL MEDIA

Between 2007 and 2012 I wrote a regular column for the Brighton based magazine Kemptown Rag. The editors at the time, the late Sarah Hall and later Kenton Hadley gave me free reign to write what I liked. Jenny featured a few times and these columns are reproduced here.

UNREQUITED. LOVE LETTER FROM THE HEART

It began with a look, a casual glance across the crowded playground. A brush back of the long dark hair, the smile, to melt the frozen paths of even the coldest of winter's mornings.

It continued with the walk and the getting to know you conversation. Her name, Jenny.

Nervous laughter and over talked sentences as the exchange for information became paramount on the short walk to our destinations. At the crossroads, Jenny took a sharp left and I continued on and on. The text came through shortly after "It was nice talking to you Russell lets do it again sometime, Jenny"

A little later, its half term. My son and I are cycling through the park, there; ahead of us, there she is, the blue-eyed beauty, with her son. "Hello", she smiles. We stop. The two boys play enjoying the slide and climbing frames. Jenny and I sit down and talk, it's natural and relaxed. I am home.

We take more walks in the park, the two boys in tow, deep in the world of childhood games, for children the fantasies take over and another world is created. A trait that never leaves us. Jenny and I laugh; I feel I have entered my little world. I don't want to leave.

A trip to the cinema. The boys eat the popcorn. Jenny and I sit close together, she passes me a chocolate and we commit the number one crime of talking in the movie house. Hushed whispers in the darkness, back and forth, competing with the soundtrack. Suppressed laughter, she rests her head on my shoulder and I fall in love.

We sit in her flat. The boys tuck into pizza and are talking about the latest Harry Potter film. They go to play outside and, at twilight, light sabres invigorate the setting winter sun.

The wine is poured and we talk and talk. It feels right, the time to confess as I look into the pale blue eyes. I tell some, but not all. I speak of the attraction I feel. I want to take the friendship further. I wait, she looks and time stops, just for that briefest of moments. Again, she looks, turns away and looks back. A brush back of the hair "Yes, I'd like that but; can we start as friends first?" My heart skips a beat and a part of me is lost forever.

Another day and the conversations continue, confidences are exchanged, the talk is effortless and, each time we part, I don't want to go, I never wanted to go, for me, always so much to talk about, so much that I wanted to say.

"Do you mind if we cancel, I am a little tired tonight" The planned supper never takes place, no more conversation, we don't make eye contact, and Jenny looks away as I walk away from her door. Something has gone. The next day I send Jenny a text to see if she is okay. Nothing in return. Soon, we meet in the playground, she smiles politely, a smile to match the skill of the most accomplished politician. It gives nothing away. She walks off, but, she doesn't leave my heart.

Time goes on and we continue to see other but, as if we are mere acquaintances. It causes me to question myself, what did I do wrong? From a near intimacy, a stranger on the walk to the playground reduces me to a passer by. I stand and look at a woman I adore who just by her being there, for me, makes the world a better place.

The feelings don't subside. A sense of loss and the feeling of something wasted. I need to tell her how I feel, a love letter from the heart.

I post the letter through her door. I tell all, how I'm crazy about her, "I'm in love with you Jenny, if you don't want to make the leap I understand, tread softly, for you tread on my dreams. I will go away with happy memories of just having been privileged to know you"

I wanted a sense of closure I thought to myself. Just to know. The hours went by then the days. The letter was never acknowledged. A letter from the heart was ignored but I had done the right thing, I had taken the ultimate risk to break out of the comfort zone. I miss Jenny. I wish her well. I wrote a letter and I was true to myself and for that, I am proud.

So, all done and I get on with life. And I do, writing the letter helps and writing the column helps more. Gradually over the coming months the feelings fade. I see Jenny occasionally, we briefly discuss the letter, "Oh, Russ, I told you I don't want a relationship, I'm sorry I thought I made that clear?" This time she has and I do feel a sense of closure and when we do meet things are easier; we actually begin to talk as friends, meeting at school sports days etc, the occasional cup of coffee.

Time moves on, life moves on and during the early months of 2009 Jenny is in touch again, we meet in the park, she is looking tired, one day as my son Leo and I are washing the car she and Oscar turn up just to say "hello". This confuses me somewhat, this time she is making the moves? Later we meet at a party and she looks strained, her sapphire blue eyes masked by darkness. As the wine flows I let down my guard and ask her round to dinner, she agrees, a few days later she turns up and for the first time I begin to feel concerned. Jenny up to this point was always immaculately turned out but as she walked into my house that evening I notice more of this gradual change for the worse. Her hair is unkempt, no make up she is wearing her glasses as if she has lost interest in life and more importantly, herself. Her comments are often negative during that evening "Oh, you're living, I'm not!" "I don't have a life anymore!" She has been made redundant from the NHS job and it appears as if the pressures of life, work and being a single mother have built up.

A few weeks later Jenny tries to take her own life. She is saved by friends, she is hospitalised and is out of touch as she later recovers with her mother. She makes a full recovery and as she does so she gets back in touch for a slow burn of a friendship turning into....I let my guard down and respond to her unexpected interest. It takes us a while and the rest as they say is history. We embark on our life journey together.

During that snow filled happiness of early 2010 I write another Cook's World which I dedicate to Jenny. When it is published she cuts it out from the magazine and frames it in the bathroom, just above the toilet. I've had worse reviews!

THAT'LL DO

Quiet pervades as I open the front door. I am blinded by the white. Dawn is creeping through the grey skies fighting for precedence with the large round flakes of snow that have appeared breaking their cloud cover. Big fluffy slippers on my feet and wrapped in my dressing gown I descend into the comforting softness of God's winter carpet. To the top of the garden I walk and look out onto the surrounding fields and roads, no grey roads, no green fields just white as far as the eye can see. Just white basking in the silence of the departing night.

The country is on hold; time stands as still as we do. Day to day life is pushed into the background as the exited voices of adults and children alike break the crispness of the morning air. Delighted footsteps not quite eclipsing the laughter of the eager children perhaps seeing the winter wonderland for the first time. Not quite eclipsing the laughter of adults thinking back to times of their own childhood, no, my childhood, the snow and the sheer bliss I remember of Jack Frost the Snowman coming to life, old bowler hat, battered brolly and carrot for a nose. Thanks Dad, do you remember? But you are not here anymore. My turn now as I leave the memory of snow filled winters of thirty five years ago. Back in the house, and pull the curtains back in my son's bedroom. The sheer colour of the dazzling whiteness lights up his face and he is awake with a look of wonder and awe.

Clothes thrown on, warm shoes found, gloves pulled on at the same time as the door is flung open, shouts of glee as he jumps into the outside, crashing into the sound of the scrunched silence of a world that today, has no school, just fun fun fun. Endless fun as I find myself smiling now dressed and running with him up the lane, breathless, hand in hand towards the park, past other parents and awe struck children, crunching through the snow breathing in the rush of cold, fresh air.

It is mid morning and the sun has lit up the white of the winter's day with a dazzling brightness that a perfect summer could never achieve. Layers of snow rest in the branches of the trees that surround the park as if settled in the gentle caress of a lovers embrace. We are there, at last, us and like dozens of others, are scattered across the hidden green like candles decorating the icing of the ultimate birthday cake.

Gleeful children take the lead as the first snowball is thrown. As each one kisses the air flying freefall, icy flakes in the sky, the smiles turn into laughter creating the community spirit that shines through when real life is pushed into the background. Through the barrage of snowballs and half built snowmen, proud Dads arrive, with hastily built toboggans pulling them across the snow, keen to demonstrate the building prowess, talents hidden for so long. A dash to the hilly slopes at the edge of the park and one two three, here we go. Rickety wooden home built machines zoom down the slopes in unison, win , the race to win, go on, you can do it, ignore the snapping sounds of the pieces of wood as the trusted DIY skills of the confident parent are tested to the very limit. There is no real winner as toboggans come to a halt to the rousing sounds of applause, the whole village is out to cheer and whoop. Fantastic.

The hours pass by in this unreal haze of snow ridden bliss, nature takes its course and soon, just as daybreak became the dawn those precious few hours ago, darkness descends and captures us all. The night can't hide that comforting blanket of frozen rain that has lead to laughter, excitement, friendship and a life spirit that would light up even the darkest of corners.

We walk home back to the world of missed calls unanswered emails and unfinished homework, our tired feet having left frozen footprints in a day of our own making. Opening the door the heat of our warm home contrasts with the cold of the outside world. As we warm up and drink the inevitable hot drinks I think back on this day, one in a million but unique as inevitably every experience is. The cold of the outside world? I don't think so. The big freeze thaws the hearts of young and old. On a day that breaks from the norm, we all pull together; we all get together and celebrate what life is all about. A kind and steady heart with a steadfast smile can make a snowy grey sky blue. Leave the doubts and fears at home, take someone's hand break into a run and look from me to you. That'll do. (For Jenny. Just because....)

In February 2011 Jenny suffers a relapse; it is unexpected and for a few days as mentioned in Aftermath, stays with me. Oscar stays with his Gran. She is lost and doesn't want to be here. "I don't want to die Russ, but the pain is too much" She takes that overdose when I am downstairs. Was it fate that I woke her later that afternoon? I had no idea she had done anything until she confessed all later saying she would understand if I want nothing more to do with her. As she battles the illness over the next few weeks Cook's World again becomes my outlet for my reply, the underlying message of not wanting our journey to stop.

WHILE YOU WERE SLEEPING

I wake and hear her breathing beside me. I look at the clock, 4.45 am. In my sleepy haze I see her lying there, peaceful, no furrowed brow and I want to take her in my arms and tell her it will all be all right. I reach out and gently stroke her face. She moves slightly as if to sit up, I pull away and watch her sleep, her long dark hair lit up by the rapidly departing moonlight as it seeps through the blinds.

I get up; a cup of tea, not too early, dawn is nearly here. The kettle whistles itself into a frenzy as I stand motionless in the kitchen, what is that noise? No, not the kettle but outside, the barking. It's constant. She needs to sleep and I want to shoot the damn dog. Things are getting to me and with the Dawn Chorus chanting, I apologise, maybe the mysterious dog hears me, it stops. The birds tweet their approval and that is good. Hopefully the approval came with the recommended use of characters...

At the kitchen table I sit and take a sip of tea. Okay, what to do. Time is on my side to go out for a little while; nothing beats a little early morning exercise. Should I stay or should I go? I tread softly as I once asked her to do so as not to shatter my dreams. I open the bedroom door. She looks at peace as I look at my world lying there. Again, my heart skips a beat and that part of me is still lost forever. Selfishly I think of myself, I need her so much, she makes my world a better place but she's not here right now.

I go out, and I deliberately don't look back to the kitchen table. There sits two bottles of pills. She takes the recommended doses, each morning as regular as clockwork. She has to, it balances things out, controls, brings a much needed clarity and when it does she gives me that smile that on our first meeting could melt the frozen paths of even the coldest of winter mornings. It still does.

Dawn rises in the fields, I watch the sunrise conscious of the fact that I should be at home but hey, once before I had taken the ultimate risk and broken out of my comfort zone, not the same but a walk would be okay? Past her flat I go, empty now and I think back to our respective sons and a twilight long gone, light sabres invigorating a setting winter sun. On I go forever forward, but the present thoughts do not go.

I can't help thinking back "Can you hang on a minute?!" she said as we sit in the car outside the local shop. "I need to get something, just to help me sleep." She looks troubled and I can't say no. She is but a couple of minutes and looks at peace when she gets back in the car. Later she looks at peace before I wake her up. A little groggier that usual but she listens as she gets up, a little unsteady as she grabs her coat. I take her back to her Mum's where she is staying temporarily if I am away, just until things settle down.

The empty bottle of pills on the bedside table should have told me all I needed to know, but it happens to other people, we just read about it don't we? "It happens to other people" I kept thinking as she confessed all two days later when I was back. She needed to talk; "the pain was too much I'm so sorry" she said as she held my hand waiting for me to shrug it off and walk away.

I don't walk away; I won't go away "with happy memories of just having been privileged to know you." The time is not right, there is so much more to do, for both of us to do together. It is not unrequited this is more than a love letter from the heart.

My pace quickens as I get towards the river, I breathe in the fresh air with the sun rising in front of me. Along the pathways and up the hills I go, memories flood back to the dog walks past and present, the times I stopped to really look. In my mind's eye I see Olivia and Stan charging ahead up to the crest, full of the joys, the exhilaration, two golden retrievers without a care in the world just enjoying life, time that cannot be captured, sheer happiness at the run and the race to catch the moment, never to be repeated . There will be more moments like this to come; I have to tell her, it is worth it. Really.

Past the river, I run up through the village and thoughts are rushing through my mind, I can't lose her, she is lost she has gone but temporarily. I need to get home. She walked away before but never left my heart but now wants to leave a whole lot more. This is wrong, it happens to other people, it happens every day but not to us and not now.

As I run I hear myself shouting internally, "I miss you, please don't go. You are better than that, we can beat this" I am babbling but what I say is true, she can't go, she has dreams of chasing rainbows at the end of the yellow brick road. I will hold her hand as we guide each other through this A-Z of life. I slow my pace as I approach the house. I push open the door and lay my key quietly on the table. Shrugging off my coat I go upstairs and I think she is still sleeping, her face turned towards the window captured by the morning sunlight. I turn to go but..." Hello, did you enjoy the walk?" "You knew I had gone? " I uttered? "Of course", she said, laughing "you had to go but if you knew I was awake?" The unanswered question....

I laughed, not the suppressed laughter of our once hushed talks in the cinema during the times of uncertainty in those unrequited days but the laughter of now. She laughs to and there is nothing quite as pretty, warm as the sunlight bringing to life summer flowers.

I take her hand; I am home where I belong where we belong. We walk downstairs and make cups of tea sitting waiting at the kitchen table for the kettle to boil. We look towards the bottles of pills and I squeeze her hand. She understands and we look out of the window to the start of a new day.

(For you...XX)

However the journey does eventually stop but the words keep on flowing. I am not a big social networker but I post my tribute to Jenny on Facebook.

NEVER AGAIN

You took that last journey on your own never again to see the light of a beautiful morning. Never again would you smile into the gentleness of a summer breeze or take a breath at the wonders of life that have eluded you for so long.

As life ebbed away and the water engulfed your physical body and the darkness unclenched its grip

219

on your soul releasing it to the warmth of eternity, never again will you wake. Never again will you lean over to me in the stillness of the night and wrap you arms around mine to feel the warmth of two bodies entwined together, never again will you hear me utter "It'll be all right", words of comfort blocked from your soul by that engulfing pain you endured for so long.

Never again will you walk through the lanes of Brighton with me, watch a sunrise, cook a meal, and snuggle up on the sofa and talk. Never again will you take me by the hand and tell me to stop being a twit or gently rub moisturiser into my cycle ridden face. Never again will we sit in our favourite pub in Exeter as I order yet another pint and you tut tut saying I drink too much. Never again will we walk round the supermarket aisles with you gently touching my hand just to make sure. Yes just to make sure if the crowds get a little too much.

Never again will we meet in town keep in contact by those so many texts. Never again will we drink those spicy coffees in the middle of the day when I should have been working; never again will I leave the house and turn back to see you in the doorway radiated by that beautiful smile. Never again will we sit snuggled up in the cinema as I feed you chocolates uttering hushed words as we hold hands tightly safe, always safe.

Never again will we sit still together and I will tell you that I love you, gazing into those anxiety ridden sapphire blue eyes. And for that brief moment as those words are spoken the darkness releases its grip and I'm there with you again and it's wonderful.

You climbed the stairs closed the door and the decision had already been made. Your final act. Never again to be reversed. You've gone physically you slipped away never again to let me pick you up and bring you back, never again just to let me … just to let me.

Never again will I open the door to see you, long dark hair pushed back to reveal the beauty of you. The conversations we should be having, the laughter we should be hearing. It's gone and I don't know what to do. Please come back….

Jenny and I spent many a happy day In Brighton. On our last visit just two weeks before she died, we both began to see the signs of the illness beginning to take its grip. It was quick this time and Jenny took the only way out that the illness offered her. As a final tribute to her now that she is really sleeping, Cook's World makes a comeback.

NOW THAT YOU ARE SLEEPING

The sun is out and we are eating our salads. We sit on a wall at the edge of Brighton Beach, the pier rising up before us. Jenny is quiet, thoughtful, and almost reflective as she munches. For a few seconds I worry that; no I gently touch her hand, she turns and smiles as if knowing what I am thinking. "I'm okay, now stop fretting and eat your lunch!" I do, we do, no dark clouds in the sky today.

The sun is out and we have finished our salads. "Come on!" says Jenny brushing back her long dark hair as she looks me directly in the eye. Immediately I am blinded, not by the sun but by the brightness of her sapphire blue eyes, clear and fresh, sparkling with life. "Come on what?" I say brandishing my plastic fork which has successfully pierced that final piece of cous cous covered pasta. "Oh you twit! I want a stroll along the pier, I want some candy floss, I want a stick of rock, with Brighton written all the way through it, lets go!" Jenny grabs my hand and we walk across the beach, the crunch of stone and shingle competing with the steady push of the Brighton tides. Always hand in hand we move along the pier, past the shops, past the amusements, we get the rock, we munch on the floss and we look at the fairground type rides. "Have they really paid money to do that?" she exclaims as we watch the gyrating swing seemingly leave Earth's atmosphere disappearing into the clouds before arriving back with a swoosh that has the girders of the resolute pier screeching with concern, just for a second. We don't gasp in amazement but walk off down the pier, so much more to do.

The sun is out and we are exploring the Lanes. They always draw us back when we are in Brighton, the perfect place to shelter from the clouds that have a habit of appearing when you least expect it. Jenny is in a mischievous mood in fact she is feeling positively tickled as we go shopping, we reach Ship Street, and we step across the threshold of the blue fronted shop, all polite smiles as we survey the array of merchandise on display, in cabinets, on tables, across the walls a panorama of toys but certainly not for the 'r us" brigade. Jenny chats animatedly with the staff, I walk around wiping the unexpected sweat from my brow and answer "no" to the question as to whether I have seen the sequel to "Who Framed Roger Rabbit?" I didn't know there was one. Jessica who? I take a step outside for some fresh air and let my imagination wander, thoughts getting lost amongst the vibrancy of the lanes. Jenny appears by my side, "Come on! I fancy some lunch!" she gives me that smile that will always melt the paths of even the coldest of winter mornings grabbing my hand as she does so. We disappear into the crowds. My beautiful lady is positively bursting with energy; I am pleased to see her so well despite the occasional cloud on the horizon. A little later as we are in the queue of a well known restaurant franchise surveying the menu, Jenny puts her arm though mine and pulls me close. "Hey" she whispers in that sensual way that always leaves me immobile with the love I feel for her "I'm really hungry can I have a foot long one please?" I blush as she slides her hand into my trouser pocket. "Have you got enough?" she winks at me. I'm flustered. "Enough what?" I say. Jenny giggles "Loose change you twit, what did you think I meant?" She orders her submarine sandwich and loudly asks for a good squirt of mayonnaise. I burst out laughing; outside in the sunshine I wrap my arms around her waist and hold her close. Each time I do so, I'm home. I like being at home.

The sun is out but I feel a little tense as we walk along King Street; we dodge the cyclists and read the billboards. What to do on this next visit? A ghost tour, a trip to the Aquarium, shows at The

Theatre Royal? I make plenty of suggestions, Jenny smiles but I sense she has other things on her mind. She is quiet as if looking to me for guidance, I pull her closer and we clearly see the possibility of a change in the weather.

The sun is out but there is a chill wind in the air, the clouds are gathering. We walk along the promenade and Jenny holds my hand a little too tightly. "How are you feeling?" I ask looking directly ahead. I feel her fingers tightening more round my hand. "Not good Russ, I am really cold and so tired can we go back to the car please?" We continue walking and as we do so a black dog runs past us and stops in front of Jenny and gives her a knowing look. Shaken, she quickly looks away and stares out to sea. The clouds now properly gather and a few minutes later as we drive away towards the coastline of Shoreham the sun goes.

The sun is out and I reach to take Jenny's hand, I want to feel the warmth of her skin touch mine but I don't, I can't and my hand remains empty. I want to turn round and to see her running towards me, laughing, long dark hair flowing behind her as she tumbles into my arms, never to leave. I stay staring straight ahead as if frozen in the moment. Jenny has gone, the dark clouds were relentless in their pursuit and this time didn't let her go.

The sun is out and I don't know what to do.

(For Jenny always, the funniest, feistiest, sexiest woman I have ever known. Asleep now and free of the dark clouds)

And so it ends. I look at the photos around me and am still dazzled by her smile and the vitality that she always showed, her love of life, her laugh, and the sheer joy I felt whenever I took her hand. Jenny died of an illness that she couldn't control, a disease of the mind that like a cancer can strike at any time. She battled so hard fought to the end but sometimes life has other plans....

CASTLES IN THE SKY

Monday 27th June 2011

"Come on Russ; wake up time for a walk!" My sly doze in the bar of the Devon based Saunton Sands hotel is interrupted. I open my eyes to see Jenny all fresh faced and wide eyed sitting next to me. "I've just sat down, a walk, where?" I reply.

Jenny takes my hand, "Just look, there, through the window, isn't it beautiful?" I shake myself out of my sleepy haze and take in the view, and I understand what she means. From the confines of the hotel bar I see past the lounge and look to the left of my eye line. There they are, a rolling cavalcade of grassy grey sand dunes stretching as far as the clichéd eye can see. I look straight ahead and down the long hill to the beach the sea is quiet just seeping onto the calm endless stretches of sand. "Peaceful, definitely" I think to myself as I turn to pick up my pint. Its not there! Then I spy Jenny chatting animatedly to the bar staff before striding purposely over to me, by that I know she is on a mission! "Your pint is quite safe; they are looking after it until we get back" she says as if anticipating my next question. "Back from where?" I ask with the indignation of a man who has done a lot of driving so clearly deserves a sit down and severe liquid refreshment! "To the beach twit, it looks so beautiful down there I want to take some photos and have a paddle, come on, are you man or mouse?" she laughs pushing her long dark hair away from her face, eyes full of mischief competing with the big grin. I get up "man or mouse eh?" I think to myself, ignoring the cheesy nibbles sitting temptingly on the table in their entire calorie trapping glory. "Right, come on, let's go!" I say with all the enthusiasm of the most dedicated of explorers and with a last wistful look towards the bar, I take Jenny's hand and we make our way to the cliff top pathway.

It's all downhill and despite a mini battle with the gorse bushes pervading the pathway we reach the beach in record time, onto the sand we walk. We stop and take in the view. The rush of the sea sliding closer and closer across the damp grey sand is captured by Jenny's camera. Click. Click, memories digitally recorded, frozen in time. Long stretches of beach, empty expanses, not a soul to be seen. Just Jenny and me, in the moment. Actually this is rather nice, there is something magical about the West Country, a slower pace, we are always rushing around, often living a life gets in the way of having a life….

The silence is only broken by the gentle brush of the sea onto the endless stretch of the beach. I breathe in the deep fresh air and start to walk. "Where are you going?" enquires Jenny as if surprised at my sudden desire for early evening exercise. "Well, I though you wanted a walk?" "Nah" she replies, "I'm cold and fancy a sip of your pint, off we go, back up the hill" she says striding purposely off towards the ominously sloping footpath, grabbing my hand as she does so.

Just as we approach the path the sun comes out, we look up towards the hotel which sits majestically above us, giving the impression of a Castle, stretching high up into the sky.

We stop as the sunlight covers the hotel. "Wow!" look at that!" she exclaims "that is beautiful! Russ, one day we must come back here, when the boys are older, we could live somewhere like this, just you and me, in our own castle in the sky?" I squeeze Jenny's hand in agreement and don't say anything and we continue walking up the hill to our temporary castle. We have all the time in the world don't we?

EPILOGUE: BACK TO THE FUTURE

The scrunching of my feet on the stony gravel produces a flurry of barks as I approach the wooden gate. As I turn the corner I see the three Golden Retrievers front paws up on the gate edge eager faces betraying their innermost thoughts, "The happy walking man is here!!" they bark in unison. I lean over and Stan drags the cap off my head, as he does every time without fail. A Britain's Got Talent contestant in the waiting. He runs around the garden pursued by the younger of the males Jerry as they fight for precedence of ownership over the old saggy cloth cap. I open the gate and Olivia with tale wagging ambles over and looks up, large doleful black eyes gazing into my soul "Are we?" the look in the eyes says it all. I pick up the leads that lie on the grass to the left of the gate. As I do so Stan bounds over and sits directly in front of me. He knows I attach the lead then another and one more. They know. Tales wagging, gate open and we are away into the familiar wilderness of the river walk.

Strides forward, strides forward and the sun is out and I know what to do. It's easy, I let the three canines off the leads, starter's orders and they are off. In my left hand I have my constant companion the Cavalier Hiking Pole, a little battered now but indispensable. I watch the dogs as they almost gallop into the distance, negotiating the pathways come rain or shine.

Dawn broke a few hours ago and as before on more lonely and contemplative walks my pace quickens but this time, I stop and take a minute to look around me. The river flows, the trees billow in the breeze, and the long grass, exaggerated in its greatness by the heavy rain both internally and externally of the past few months, waits for the patter of Golden Retriever heavy paws. Nature is not disappointed as they trundle past in a flurry of fur, excitement and general lust for life, charging down their own yellow brick road into the new sunshine of a much delayed summers day. They know what to do.

I watch them bound off into the distance and I smile broadly as the sunlight floods across the ground like that smile of someone who is still very much a part of me that could melt the paths of even the coldest of winter's mornings. I don't feel cold any more and I am glad that the sun is out again.

Just before we make our way back home; I throw a stick into the glistening river, Olivia jumps in; splash! She pulls it from the water and resolutely refuses to let it go turning her head away as I reach for it so we can play again. Silly how can we continue to play the game? She never understands. The sound of my laughter echoes alongside the running water as I watch Stan and Jerry join us from their travels over hill and dale. They drink deeply from the river and are immediately invigorated. They know what to do.

Home and Leo is waiting for me, he looks the three dogs up and down. "Been swimming again have they Daddy?" We both smile as we towel the dogs down; they sit like three expectant members of royalty being waited on by their entourage. Yep, they know what to do.

"Right are you ready young man?" Leo looks at me momentarily confused. "Ready for what?", my son asks, curiously. "Well, I promised you and Oscar a pizza evening so guess what, I have bought all the ingredients. Prepare to be amazed for a home made pizza of epic proportions with toppings to thrill and amaze your taste buds!"My son looks at me incredulously as we walk towards the car, "Are you sure you know what you are doing?" he asks with all the tact of a twelve year old who has expertly memorised the opening times of the nearest Dominos store.

I think for a moment then look him directly in the eye. "Yes, yes I do" I say smiling and we drive home. I like home.

The two key players in this story are the boys, Oscar and Leo. Back in 2012 they were not that close. If things had developed as Jenny and I had talked we would have eventually have got married and immediately from not that good friends to stepbrothers. Drawn together through tragic circumstances, they have over the years become incredibly close. That friendship has developed to encompass a wider circle of mutual friends developed through school and college. The ties are strong and this stretches through to a strong union that has developed again between Oscar and Avril. Avril has known him since he was two when she and Jenny were neighbours. Her strength, loyalty and kindness know no bounds, so much so that Oscar has added her surname by deed poll to his own. Add to this various members of Avril's immediate family especially her niece Caroline. She and Oscar are the same age and have grown up together. Seeing them together, two complete opposites who have the closest of brother and sister relationships.

Oscar has also formed a brother like relationship with Avril's now eight year old son. He was born a few months before Jenny died. As he has grown so has Oscar, by his side.

The family unit that Avril has provided has become even more important since his Gran Belinda passed away in her sleep in February 2019. She was just shy of her eightieth birthday. When her daughter died she immediately took Oscar under her protective wing and supported and nurtured him though his teenage years, never a word of complaint. In life the phrase "tough as old boots" would be an understatement. She was formidable! Time spent with Belinda was never to be forgotten. Uncompromising, outspoken and all in all rather wonderful!

Leo's Mum and my ex wife has been to me the best friend anyone can have. The support especially in the early days she gave most importantly to her son but also to me which has continued to this day has been fantastic. A level of support that I can never repay. No greater friend.

The grief and the questions will always be with us. This past year though feels different as if the past is accepting itself and letting us move on. Doors are closing but not in a bad way and this past New Years Eve, Avril, Oscar, Leo and I had a wonderful evening drinking and reminiscing especially about

Jenny and some of the mad escapades we had all been on with her. What is sometimes forgotten when you are dealing with this illness is the person, the person who once was. Jenny was a feisty vibrant lady who enjoyed life wit a quirky outlook reflected in her sense of humour. She was naturally inquisitive always up for an adventure and having fun and quality time with friends. We spent the evening looking at the positives. Emotional yes but boy did we laugh as the alcohol flowed. It really was as we saw in 2020 a case of Should Old Acquaintance be not forgotten!

The pain never goes away but it is manageable, time doesn't heal but it gives you opportunities. It took me a long while to realise this, being in the same house with all this history is not I can assure you good for the mental health. You get cocooned with a set of memories, stuck unable to move on, you don't realise it at the time. This led to my own battles with mental health. I had some low times. The knots were untied by the outside, regular exercise, I started Spin classes at the Leisure centre which introduced me to a new group of friends.

Special mention to the three Golden retrievers whose presence has featured through this narrative. Since 2008 Stan and Olivia have been my constant companions on the Itchen Way River

Walk. In 2010 we were joined by their son Jerry. Owned by Leo's Mum they are my step dogs and time with them in the open air has been the saving and making of me. They have taught me about living in the moment, the power of silence as we walk the fields and just being.

Now we finish. I look out into my garden which has also come a long way in the past few years. In 2012 a mess of weeds, rubbish an overgrowth of nothing.

Things took a turn for the better when I planted a Japanese maple. It was tagged an "Acer Orange Dream". When I bought this twig like plant it didn't look like it would survive the day let alone take route in the soil, grasp life and grow, across the weeks, months and years. It has survived the frostbite of winters, the torrential rain of wet and windy springs, the unforgiving Autumnal winds and going on to glory and blossom in the basking warmth of some long hot summers. Now it takes pride of place by the back door, a shining light amongst the colour of the plants that I have cultivated as companions for the maple.

On a summers evening I sit with the vibrant colour of the chrysanthemums, geraniums, petunias, marigolds, along with the red, yellow and pink rose bushes. It all surrounds me to suppress the

236

black as I breathe in the much more colourful
atmosphere of eight years on.

The Beginning?

RECOMMENDED READING.

REASONS TO STAY ALIVE. MATT HAIG.
(Canongate £9.99)

BEING ADAM GOLIGHTLY. ADAM GOLIGHTLY
(Short Books £8.99)

IT'S OK TO FEEL BLUE. SCARLETT CURTIS (editor)
(Penguin £14.99)

HISTORY OF A SUICIDE. JILL BIALOSKY (Granta £
9.99)

JOG ON. BELLA MACKIE. (William Collins £8.99)

BLACK RAINBOW. RACHEL KELLY (Yellow Kite
Books £8.99)

AN UNQUIET MIND. KAY RADFIELD JAMISON (Picador £9.99)

MAD GIRL. BRYONY GORDON (Headline £9.99)

EAT, DRINK, RUN. BRYONY GORDON (Headline £9.99)

THINGS I LEARNED FROM FALLING. CLAIRE NELSON (Aster £ 12.99)

SANE NEW WORLD. RUBY WAX (Hodder £9.99)

MENTAL HEALTH.

This memoir is my experience of Mental Health. All treatment is different; all treatment is individual or should be tailored to the individual. If when you are suffering from this terrible disease you at the darkest of moments will rebel against any care that you are offered, the Black Dog will bark away protecting itself quite ferociously. Jenny rebelled, occasionally reducing her medication when she thought she was getting better which due to the severity of the illness sent her straight back down that dark forbidding well. Trapped, seemingly with no way out.

Each person is different, to be treated with care and understanding. If you have a broken leg then usually feet up and a rest. If you have a broken mind, then that's another matter.

For further information and help, contact your local GP. They can help and will point you in the right direction for that first tentative step towards recovery. Other avenues are:

SANE.   www.sane.org.uk/   Tel: 0203 3805 1790   Email: info@sane.org.uk

MIND. www.mind.org.uk/   INFOLINE: 0300 123 3393   Email: info@mind.org.uk

ABOUT THE AUTHOR

Russell Cook is a writer and voice-over artist. He has contributed interviews features and articles to Doctor Who Magazine, Geeky Monkey and Thame Out Magazine amongst others.

Between 2007 and 2012 he devised and wrote the Cook's World column for the Brighton based magazine Kemptown Rag.

Since 2003 he has written a book review column in AND Magazine which is read widely across the south coast. AND Magazine has also featured his interviews and profiles of Clive James, Tom Baker and Mike Brearley amongst others.

His voice talents have been featured on local radio, corporate videos and two seasons of Sky Television's World's Most Evil Killers.

His blog Brave New World can be found at http://therewriteman.wordpress.com . He lives in Hampshire

245

Printed in Poland
by Amazon Fulfillment
Poland Sp. z o.o., Wrocław

61770199R00146